UNITED NATIONS AND INDIAN MYSTICISM

By the Same Author:

1. Bankers Safety: Methods and Techniques.
2. Crime Law and Police Science

About the Author

Dr. Vadackumchery (*b.* 1949) who is an author of 47 books on crime, police and justice analyses the mystical revelations from above—the divinely inspired eternal truths—and says that the intuition of Indian mystics contains a lot of human rights. The *ṛsis* and sages experienced them much before human intellect could see them. Police is a new concept and the United Nations may be a newer concept. But, human rights are not. The mystics have a vision of the soul and precisely, therefore, for a mystic, none of the above concepts—Police, United Nations, Human Rights—could be new. Dr. Vadackumchery is a noted writer on human rights and an activist in every sense. He has specially authored two books on human rights and police. The history of India shows that she has been conquered and dominated again and again by many powers, nevertheless, her distinctive civilization, culture, philosophy or metaphysics have survived. This is because she has a heritage which accepts human rights, dignity of individual and worth of human person and the heritage is founded on mystical intuitions and revelations which cannot die if at all the Declarations and Conventions resolved by United Nations—the world community—get perished in due course. This is what is seen in the book. The contents of the book will appeal many as they give new visions on human rights—even taking away the claims which some authors make about the fatherhood of human rights.

Dr. James Vadackumchery is born at Manjapra (India) and teaches criminology at the Police Training College, Thiruvananthapuram, Kerala. His association with police officers of all ranks makes him to bring out with authority many passages and parallels on human rights and police in Indian mysticism and United Nations. Dr. Vadackumchery is frank in his treatment of the subject and he opens a new area for research on human rights.

He is married to Mary and has two daughters Neethu and Neethie.

UNITED NATIONS AND INDIAN MYSTICISM

Parallels on Human Rights and Police

JAMES VADACKUMCHERY

CONCEPT PUBLISHING COMPANY, NEW DELHI-110059

ISBN : 81-7022-664-2

First Published 2002

Published and Printed by
Ashok Kumar Mittal
Concept Publishing Company
A/15-16, Commercial Block, Mohan Garden
New Delhi-110059 (INDIA)

Phone : 5648039, 5649024
Fax : 091-11-5648053
Email : publishing@conceptpub.com

A Millennium Gift to
My wife and daughters
to
Mary
Neethu and Neethie

PREFACE

People look to the west—and to the United Nations—to know more about human rights. They do not go to the Indian scriptures and do not make attempts to discover the parallels between today's world views on human rights and the ancient Indian views on the same subject. Of course, Indian mystics never said "Human Rights", for human rights might be new words given to the ancient Indian thoughts. On going through the Indian thoughts—mysticism—I find that many of the U.N. concepts of human rights have their parallels in our own scriptures. The U.N. Declarations and Conventions, sometimes, repeat the same thing seen in ancient Indian teachings. For, ancient Indian thoughts speak of truths and truths are eternal. "There is nothing higher than truth" (*Mahabharata, Santi Parva*, 330, 10, 12) and human rights are the eternal truths and they can be realized only by having truth in human mind.

United Nations, Police and Human Rights—Do they have any relationship? Yes, they are related. For, all of them stand for justice and in *Brihadaranyaka Upanishad* (1, 4, 14), it is written "Verily that which is Justice is Truth". The United Nations have brought out a number of Conventions and all of them contain a lot of principles to guide the working of police ensuring human rights to people. In policing a society consisting mostly of their own people, the police need guidance. People all over the world see that the police are, sometimes, not human rights friendly when they interact with people and the United Nations feel it so strongly that they insist on just, truthful and human rights friendly policemen. "God protects him, who is just and truthful and destroys him who is not so" (*Ṛg* Veda, 7,104,12). The police, if they have a bad image today, have not been just and truthful in their dealings with people. For, justice and truthfulness coincide with the concepts of human rights. A just and truthful man can not but be human rights friendly.

For, the "heaven and earth sustain a justice loving man" (*Ṛg Veda*, 3, 26, 9).

Human rights have no borders and recognize no boundaries. From the birth of man, there were human rights violations and certainly some people respected the human rights in some form or other. Some form of policing was there in every society—down the millennia. Some sort of human rights violations by the police (or whatever nomenclature the police was known in ancient societies) could be seen everywhere and there were reactions to such police misbehaviour always in human history.

'*Dharma*' in Indian mysticism signified eternal laws and Indians believed that it maintained the world. '*Dharma*' also signified the obligation which a man had and his obligation constituted his duties. In that sense, I may say that the man's obligation to respect human rights and the dignity of man is his 'Dharma' in life. The opposite of '*Dharma*' is '*Adharma*' and logically, one who refuses to recognize the human rights of his fellow brethren commits '*Adharma*' in life. Police have a '*dharma*' and the *Vedas* say that the foundation of '*dharma*' is religion. Whenever an individual performs his '*dharma*', he performs a duty which is as much social as religious. Respecting the human rights of people by police is, as said above, a '*dharma*'. In *Isha Upanishad*, it is written. "They who neglect their social duties for their individual life fall in darkness; and those who sacrifice their individuality for social popularity fall into greater darkness". Article 29 of the Universal Declaration of Human Rights by the United Nations reads: "Everyone has duties to the community in which alone the free and full development of his personality is possible".

'*Brahman*' is the ultimate reality and is the 'soul' or the inner essence of every being. Manifestation of *Brahman* is seen in the human soul and it is called '*Atman*'. *Atman* is the individual and *Brahman* is the ultimate reality. Hindus believe that the *Atman* and *Brahman* are one and this in fact is the essence of *Upanishads*. When the United Nations proclaim that recognition of the inherent dignity and of equal and inalienable rights of all members of the human family, they mean the *Atman* and *Brahman* of Indian mysticism. And precisely, therefore, every human being has equal rights and dignity.

"From the unreal, lead me to the real,
From darkness, lead me to light,
From death, lead me to immortality."
(*Brihad Upanishad*)

In all proclamations and declarations by the United Nations on human rights, the people in one voice say that they want to be led—from the unreal to the real, from darkness to light and from death to immortality. United Nations want to have a common understanding of human rights and freedoms among the people and they think that such an understanding is essential for the full realizations of the pledge to enforce human rights throughout the world. This they say in the very preamble of the Universal Declaration of Human Rights and the pledge is necessary to lead people to reality, light and immortality. This becomes inevitable and in the words of United Nations:

"Whereas it is essential, if man is not to be compelled to have recourse, as a last resort, to rebellion against tyranny and oppression, that human rights should be protected by the rule of law". Thc intentions of the United Nations are very clear and they are sincere to the core.

"*Let thy speech be pure,
forceful and sweet*"
(*Atharva Veda*, 16, 2,9)

The intentions are spelt out in Article 29 of the Universal Declaration and they run as:

> "In the exercise of his rights and freedoms, everyone shall be subject only to such limitations as are determined by law solely for the purpose of securing due recognition and respect for the rights and freedoms of others and meeting the just requirements of morality, public order and the general welfare of a democratic society". Certainly, the

people of the world will reach their destination unanimously-but slowly. "With patience, gain victory over yourself" (*Ṛg Veda*, 10, 167-1) and with patience, the people will gain victory over all and themselves in the achievement of human rights—"All Rights For All".

United Nations and Indian mystic writings—they meet in the Universal Declaration of Human Rights. The parallels between the world views on human rights and mystical experiences may seem surprising and it is not the sole objective of the author to bring out the parallels between what the United Nations have proclaimed so far on human rights and what the mystics have observed through their introspection in the privacy of their meditation. The world views may be changed, but mystical thoughts seem to be the unique experiences of a blessed few at special occasions. A closer examination shows, however, that the difference between the world views and mystical experiences lie only in their approaches and not in their reliability, validity, truthfulness and eternity. Vedic texts contain revealed truths. They teach divine words received directly by the inspired bards—the *ṛsis.* The *Ṛg Veda*, the *Sama Veda*, the *Yajur Veda* and the *Atharva Veda* are revelations (*Sruti*) and certainly, they are superior to the world views which cannot but rest on revealed truths. Of course, the mystics were not talking about human rights as such, but they were revealing human truths which included, among other things, human rights. The United Nations spoke about human rights, but they spoke nothing more than what the *ṛsis* said centuries ago. The *ṛsis* conveyed "messages" ensuring the ultimate good to man and humanity and they conveyed them to all men on earth—for all times.

The author does not intend to explore and expose all the mystic experiences to all human rights proclaimed by United Nations. He confines only to human rights and police as seen in Indian mysticism and in the Declarations, Proclamations, Conventions of the United Nations. Mystics do not speak anything much about police and human rights. Nevertheless, it is possible to find out the relevance of U.N.'s Declarations on human rights to police just like one may find the relevance of Indian mystical writings on police functioning today. Any researcher can make deeper studies and find out parallels between Indian mysticism and U.N. views in other areas of human rights. All I can hope to do by this work is to generate research interests among people to an area which has been hither to uncared.

I do not claim that I am a scholar in Indian philosophy and mysticism. Of course, I studied western and eastern philosophy for three years in an academic institution. When I studied the U.N. Declarations with an emphasis on police and human rights, I had a feeling that many of the world views on human rights had their roots in Indian philosophy and mysticism. I wrote two books on police and human rights and they were (1) *Human Rights and the Police in India* (2) *Human Rights Friendly Police: A Myth or Reality*? I also edited a book titled *Police and Human Rights*. The books were received well. I had an uncontrollable urge then to explore the parallels between Human Rights and Indian Mysticism. I got in touch with some scholars in Indian Philosophy and I found that they knew a lot about Indian philosophy and mysticism. They did not know much about human rights! This compelled me to read texts on the subject and I could collect a number of parallels between human rights and Indian mystical writings. They were very exhaustive and precisely, therefore, I confined myself only to those parallels which were related to human rights and police. I do claim that this is a pioneering attempt in this area.

This book is intended for a general reader who has an interest in Indian mysticism, human rights and police. I hope to find among my readers human rights activists with an interest in the philosophical aspects of human rights and police. I hope that my readers will understand that Indian mysticism provides a strong and beautiful foundation which can accommodate our latest views on police and human rights. Of course, the contents of the book make an exposition of Indian mystical thoughts and U.N. declarations on human rights. Throughout the book, the reader's understanding of police and human rights must progress steadily, but a comparable progression in the understanding of the mystical thoughts may not occur. This seems unavoidable as the mystics were not talking about human rights and the police at that time.

Mysticism is an experience—a revelation from above and the reader has to bear this in his mind when he goes through the book. During the writing of this book, my own understanding and appreciation of Indian mystical thoughts have deepened considerably.

I am indebted to my wife, Mary and daughters, Neethu and Neethie for their assistance. I am profoundly grateful to them. The views and opinions expressed in this book are personal and they are not the views of the Government of India, State governments, police departments and home offices. Dr. James Vadackumchery hereby affirms that he has the moral rights to be identified as the author of this title. To conclude, I may quote *Dhammapada*: "They who imagine truth in untruth, and see untruth in truth, never arrive at truth and follow true desires."

Before I conclude, I wish to say that I do not and cannot make pretensions. Indian mystical revelations are mysterious in nature and I do not want to claim that I have understood them fully. When I went through the inspired truths, I had just a feeling—i.e., many of these eternal truths are what we see in the human rights declarations and conventions of the United Nations. I made attempts, afterwards, to study Indian mysticism and wanted to find out parallels to the principles of human rights seen in International Conventions and Declarations. My attempt has yielded success and thus I affirm that Indian mystical revelations are wonderful and our *ṛsis* are the ancient forefathers of Magna Carta, French and American Declarations, Universal Declaration of Human Rights and what not? It may be clarified that a good many passages are not taken from the original sources as I think that it is not necessary to do so. The intention of this research work is to expoṣe the Indian mysticism and human rights movements in the world. Very many passages, I have quoted, are carefully racked out of antologies and other books of Indian mysticism. It is not an imperfection of this book, rather is the uniqueness of this work and it will make people understand better the concepts and parallels brought out in this title.

Thiruvananthapuram Crmgst Jame Vadackumchery

CONTENTS

CONTENTS

1

Police, Human Rights and Indian Mysticism

"There is none high or low amongst you. You are all brethren and, therefore, strive all together to attain prosperity" (*Ṛg Veda* 50, 60, 5)

What a profound thought on human rights!

"Whereas recognition of the inherent dignity and of the equal and inalienable rights of all members of the human family is the foundation of freedom, justice and peace in the world".... The United Nations proclaim this in the very Preamble of their Declaration of Human Rights. The mystics in India accepted it in ancient times. "There is none high or low amongst you" and I think that it might be the earliest human rights declaration in India—in the world (?).

"As, O God, Thou art for
ever the common Lord of
all alike, as such we
invoke Thee now" (*Ṛg Veda* 4, 32, 13)

and certainly the Indians believed that all human beings have a common Lord and that is the worth of human life. Man has an inherent dignity and that is what the United Nations speak in the Preamble of the Universal Declaration of Human Rights.

"Whereas disregard and contempt for human rights have resulted in barbarous acts which have outraged the conscience of mankind, and the advent of a world in which human beings shall enjoy freedom of speech and belief and freedom from fear and want has been proclaimed as the highest aspiration of the common people" and a parallel to this thought is seen in *Manu Smriti* (4, 139) as:

> "One should always speak sweet, pleasant and agreeable words and should not utter harsh and offensive words causing dissensions and discord"

and this is what is said by the United Nations in the preamble of U.D.H.R. The policemen are, sometimes, blamed for their use of obscene words and epithets when they interact with people and certainly such a disregard and contempt for human rights of people by the policemen have resulted in branding policemen as human rights unfriendly to people. A lack of understanding of the eternal truths in the Indian scriptures is, probably, the root cause of human rights unfriendly behaviour of Indian police.

Human rights have a profound influence on almost all functionings of police today in India. They have become the basis of crime investigation and law enforcement by police. I do not think that the police were influenced by ancient Indian thoughts to have a change in their attitude and approach to human rights. The onset of human rights consciousness among the policemen and the people is traced back to 1993 when the Protection of Human Rights Act was enacted in India. Even in 1994, 1995, 1996, I could see a total resistance to human rights concepts among the policemen. Afterwards, I found a sort of passive resistance—tolerance—reluctant acceptance and finally an acceptance with murmuring and mumblings. On the other hand, the people enthusiastically embrace human rights concepts and insist for their effective implementation on a war-footing. The Protection of Human Rights Act 1993 has fundamentally changed the people's attitude to police and the police attitude to people.

'These changes were certainly beneficial and detrimental to police and people'—thus say some critics on human rights. Nevertheless, today there is hardly any police function that does not have human rights dimensions and basis on human rights. The impact or influence of the human rights consciousness extends to the realm of thought and culture of the people and the police where it has led to a deep revision in people's and police conception of the human rights world in the third millennium.

Indian Sages and Human Rights

Indian scriptures, culture, sages, *gurus* and *swamijees* recognized human rights long—very long ago. Everybody is equal to anybody and is equal in every measure—that was what the Indians upheld from time immemorial. But, the Indian voice was not loud, for they were not talking with the tongues of men using loud speakers—or by the strength of nations.

They wanted to live a life exhibiting the concept as Swami Ram Tirath said:

> "If we look through all the earth
> Men we see have equal birth
> Made in one great brotherhood,
> Equal in the sight of God, the good.
> Food or caste or place of birth
> Cannot alter human worth".

Indian sages believed in the equal birth, great brotherhood, equality in the sight of God and human worth of people. They were truths to them and they believed: "Truth alone triumphs and not untruth" (*Mundaka Upanishad* III, 1, 6). In *Mahabharata*, Yudhisthira says: "Truth is greater than power of posterity and has to be guarded at all costs". Human rights are rights of the people—inalienable and inviolable rights and eternal truths that are seen ever since man was born into the world. The United Nations have just reaffirmed this truth when they said:

> "Whereas the people of the United Nations have in the Charter reaffirmed their faith in the fundamental human rights, in the dignity and worth of human person and in the equal rights of men and women and have determined to promote social progress and better standards of life in larger freedom".

When United Nations proclaimed reaffirming the eternal truths already stated by Indian sages, people all over the world listened to them. The words of the United Nations conveyed meanings and the meanings were no different from what might be seen in *Dharma Sutra*: "One should speak the truth and speak it pleasingly; one should not speak untruth because it happens to be pleasing". The United Nations spoke the truth in a pleasing way and the intentions were to make a new world order which respects human rights and the worth of human person. They wanted to mould the society in tune with what the Indian sages wished. "Society must be moulded upon truth. Truth has not to adjust itself to society" (Swami Vivekananda).

Indian *Vedas*— *ṛsis* —conveyed to humanity—

> "All who can walk are equally
> entitled to the use of paths and roads" (*Rg Veda,* 2, 13, 2)

and it took several years—more than several millennia—for the people of the United Nations to adopt the same concept for 'promoting social progress and better standards of life in larger freedom". In article 13, U.D.H.R., the United Nations emphatically proclaimed: "Everyone has the right to freedom of movement and residence within the borders of each State".

The exploration of the human rights concepts during the latter part of the twentieth century and the insistence by the United Nations for the acceptance of human rights values by all peoples of the world have revealed an unsuspected recognition of the inviolable rights of man throughout the world. People now graciously admit that human rights recognize no boundaries and all human rights are for all under the sun—for all people—until the consumption of the world. In *Gita*, it is written:

> "I am the same in all the
> beings, neither is any dearer
> to Me nor hateful".

It implies that everyone is equal before God and everyone can enjoy equal rights. This is what the United Nations want to promote and "to reaffirm faith in fundamental human rights, in the dignity and worth of human person, in the equal rights of men and women and of nations, large and small". For this purpose, United Nations insist "to practice tolerance and to live together in peace with one another as good neighbours".

The concepts of human dignity, tolerance, living together were recognized by Indians long before—from time antiquity—even before the nations of the world thought about it—long before Magna Carta of 1215 came into being—long before the American Declaration of Rights in 1774 and the French Declaration of 1789 saw the light of the day. In *Bhavishya Purana,* we read: ".......... being the children of the same father, there is no difference of their caste or race". Castes and races worked as barriers and frustrators in human relations and inter-personnel contacts. U.N.'s Declaration on Elimination of All Forms of Racial Discrimination [Resolution 1904 (XVIII)] of November 20, 1963 puts down:

> "All are entitled to equal protection against all discrimination and against any incitement to such discrimination"

United Nations continue:

> "Discrimination between human beings on the ground of race, colour or ethnic origin is an offence to human dignity and shall be condemned as a denial of the principles of the Charter of the United Nations, as a violation of the human rights and fundamental freedoms proclaimed in the Universal Declaration of Human Rights as an obstacle to friendly and peaceful relations among nations and as a fact capable of disturbing peace and security among peoples".

Indian sages and *rsis* had the revelation of these facts and their inspired truths were solemnly proclaimed by the United Nations during the latter part of the twentieth century and many nations thus accepted the divinely inspired eternal truths for future guidance. This acceptance necessitated a radical revision of many of their earlier concepts—even those including the concepts relating to police and policing. The concept of policing a democracy, for example, is totally different from the traditional idea of policing a society by making the police as a coercive weapon of the Government in power. Today, the police are no more considered as the coercive weapon of a government in power. Police now are public servants and they are no more treated as a coercive force. They have to function in society fully respecting the human rights of people without taking into account the caste, creed, colour and community. Many new concepts like people's police, policing the society by people's participation, community policing—all for respecting the human rights of people come into being.

What is new in the so-called new concepts? Indian sages said:

> "Make no distinction between man and man just like the ripples of water which rise in water and get absorbed in it"
>
> —Gauri Kabir

United Nations could notice that discrimination based on race, colour or ethnic origin in certain areas continued amidst people causing serious concerns. In police too such discri-minatory treatment could be observed—discrimination based on political affiliations, economic positions, social status etc., was observed in police functionings. Alarmed at the differential treatment seen in police handling people, a Code of Conduct was enforced for law enforcement officers by the U.N. and for Indian Police by Government of India. Under Article 7 of the U.N. Declaration on the Elimination of All Forms of Racial Discrimination, it is stated: "Everyone has the right to equality before the law and equal justice under law". How can a law enforcement officer discriminate people?—man from man?—man from woman only on the basis of caste, race, ethnic origin etc. But people do so.

Universal Declaration of Human Rights do not speak anything directly about police and police functionings.

Nevertheless, it has direct/indirect connections with the enforcement of human rights. Indian mysticism does not, likewise, deal with police and police functionings. But, certainly the revealed truths have direct/indirect relations with the enforcement of human rights in many ways.

> "May all beings look on me with the eye of a friend; may I look on all beings with the eye of a friend. May we look on each other with the eye of a friend" (*Yajur Veda,* 26, 2).

The above mystic thought, no doubt, emphasizes the equality of man, equal rights of men and friendship among all human beings. The police are the friends of the people and the people are the friends of the police and if they look at each other as friends, certainly there will be no violations of human rights by police during law enforcement.

In order to ensure friendly relations among people and peoples, United Nations have brought out a number of international instruments on human rights, in particular the International Covenant on Economic, Social and Cultural Rights and the International Covenant on Civil and Political Rights and Optional Protocols.

Everyone's life must be human rights friendly and must be a life of sacrifice. For, one cannot ensure human rights without total dedication and sacrifice. In *Upanishads,* this concept is well written.

"Let my life be a life of dedication, let my vital breath, eyes, ears, intellect and spirit be dedicated to service; let my love and my understanding, my prosperity and my knowledge be dedicated to service. Let the service be made in a spirit of sacrifice". For this, "Education shall be directed to the full development of the human personality and to the strengthening of respect for human rights and fundamental freedoms. It shall promote understanding, tolerance and friendship among all nation's, racial and religious groups and shall further the activities of the United Nations for the maintenance of peace (*cf.* Article 26, U.D.H.R.).

What is the worth and value of human life?—particularly

when people are not prepared to respect the worth of human person? If human dignity is not accepted, then human life becomes meaningless—not worth living. All the human rights declarations become empty words and hollow utterances.

> "Let every hand give comfort to all living beings and let it be the giver of health to the whole mankind"
>
> (*Ṛg Veda,* 10-137-7).

This divine inspiration alone can give meaning to human life. The entire exercise of the United Nations centre around this sublime thought and "He who will not give finds none to comfort him" (*Rg Veda,* 10-117-1). Indian mystics had intuitive knowledge and they knew that the world moved to a state which they saw in their divine wisdom. U.N. Declarations and activities are nothing but the extensions of the inspired—mystical—teachings.

Ṛsis, sages and Indian mystics appealed to human courts and man's conscience to enforce the eternal truths for the common good of mankind. The United Nations sought for international co-operation and established international bodies for enforcing human rights laws. Dr. S. Radhakrishnan, the President of India in 1963 appealed to the nations of the world to surrender a part of their sovereignty to a central world authority. To quote President, Dr. Radhakrishnan:

> "What is essential today, if we wish to bring about a human community, a world community, is to surrender a part of our sovereignty to a central authority, to do our utmost to remove the injustices which prevail in the name of colonial subjection, in the name of racial segregation, in the name of economic exploitation, in the name of even religious tolerance. These are the things which must be removed. It is easy to win peace, but we would also win the conditions which make for peace. These conditions are that we should not adhere to the kind of heritage which has come down to us. We must respect the past for the sake of the future. The

hope of the world lies in our trying to exceed, transcend outmoded nationalist attitude. They have their place so far as cultural expression is concerned. But they have no place if you think that every nation is the supreme sovereign of its own way of life and that it can fight others in the name of its particular way of life. That attitude has to be given out."

President Dr. Radhakrishnan in his address to the Council of Asian Relations and World Affairs said emphatically: "This is an age of interdependence, and our way is clear. We must surrender a part of our sovereignty, work together for the elimination of every kind of injustice wherever we find it. Injustice must hurt you as much as it hurts the people who suffer from it. If you have a sensitive conscience, you will feel that those people who are hungry, who are poor, whose lives are inhibited, are a challenge to us all; and so long as they exist, it will not be possible for us to develop a real human community."

The Indian President continued: "We must have this sense of world community which we must give our young people, our students, in the plastic years of their lives. You must make them feel that they all belong to one human family. There is no such thing as this nation or the nation superseding the claims of the human community. If the two things come into conflict, you must sacrifice your own sovereignty."

Indian sages, down the centuries, have been talking with the tongues of human rights. Perhaps the Indian *sadhus* and holy men have spoken more about the worth of human person than many others in the entire world. "Him I call *'Mahatma'* whose heart bleeds for the poor, otherwise he is a *"Duratma"*—said Swami Vivekananda. What more do the people need to become compassionate to others than these secret thoughts? Swami Vivekananda repeatedly exhorted:

"Our duty to others means
helping others doing good
to the world"
"Take up an idea. Make
that idea your life;

think of it; dream of it;
live on it"

and the ideas of human rights, human freedom, human dignity, human tolerance and mutual acceptance must certainly, be taken up and they must be made the ideas of everyone's life and they must be enforced—or—the people must live on them.

In Appendix of this book, I have listed out the United Nation's standards and norms in crime prevention and criminal justice. In the world views expressed by the United Nations, it is seen—

— Being deeply concerned…
— Affirming…
— Observing…
— Believing…
— Feeling …
— Calls upon …
— Urges…
— Recommends …
— Bearing in mind …
— Considering …
— Recalling …
— Inviting …
— Acknowledging …
— Welcoming …
— Emphasizing …
— Adopting …
— Aware of …
— Mindful …
— Convinced …
— Concerned …
— Alarmed at …
— Requesting … etc.

and they emphasize the need for enforcing human rights of people. A study of Indian mysticism, it may be further noted, may convince us all that the mystics have already had the intuitive vision of everything which the United Nations speak and others follow now. United Nations want international co-operation and mutual assistance in enforcing human rights, personal dignity and freedoms. Look into the mystical teachings of Indian sages and there one sees all these facts, perhaps, in a more profound way than what they are seen in the world views today.

"Whoever is kind to the creation, God is kind to him, therefore, be kind to man on the earth whether he be good or bad, and being kind to the bad is to withhold them from badness" (*Hadis*) and this is what is taught by human rights laws on the attitude and approach to be taken towards the suspects, arrestees, detinues, accused and so on by police. No torture, no coercion, no humiliation, no victimization, no harassment to crime doers, for, they are against the principles in human rights.

"There is no honey like politeness and no poison like impoliteness. Civility is a cool and sweet drink and uncivility is the worst poison. Courtesy affords peace while discourtesy causes impairment. Gentleness makes difficult things easy, while rudeness makes easy things difficult" (Kabit Bhai Gurdas). The Indian literature contains, thus, a number of noble thoughts which are directly or indirectly related to human rights. Nevertheless, it is not the aim of this book to bring such sublime teachings here.

Mystic revelations and United Nations want to eradicate evils from the world and they want to establish peace and harmony.

"Evils must be eradicated promptly, for a thorn which has been allowed to remain in the body may cause a pestering wound" (*Mahabharata*). Human rights violations are evils in society and if they are committed by any one, particularly the police who are to enforce them, then it is like the protectors becoming annihilators. United Nations, by promoting human rights, want to establish world harmony and international co-operation for human development. Unity is necessary for enforcing human rights in the world and unity is essential to administer justice by police in a human rights friendly way.

Just see what is said in *Ṛg Veda*.

> "Be united; speak in harmony; let your minds apprehend alike; common be your prayer; common be the end of your assembly; common be your resolutions; common be your deliberations; unified be your hearts; common be your intentions, perfect be your unity" (*Rg Veda* 10, 191, 24).

Most unfortunately, many do not absorb the ideas conveyed through the mystical revelations as they think that they are not related to human rights. I met a professor of Indian Philosophy. He was a Sanskrit scholar who had authored a book on 'Mysticism'. I felt happy and I asked him to tell me something or anything about Indian mysticism and human rights. Honestly, he confessed to me that he did not have any reading on human rights. The concept of human rights, it seemed to me, was Greek to him; nevertheless, he told me a lot about Indian mystical revelations. When he spoke to me about Indian mysticism, I thought about Socrates who was made to say in Plato's dialogue called the Symposium: "The curse of ignorance is that a man without being good or wise is nevertheless satisfied with himself; he has no desire for that of which he feels no want". How can a professor of philosophy and an author of mysticism be satisfied with himself if he does not know the ABC of human rights? These professors must proclaim to the world everything which the Indian sages did tell about human rights. The pity today is that many people and nations father or godfather the concepts on human rights. Indian mystical revelations do not get what they ought to have got from the international community, and the most important reason for it, I think, is the lack of interest or the ignorance which the authors on mysticism have in exposing the relationship between human rights and Indian mystical teachings.

As seen in any culture in the world, human rights violations were found in ancient India as well. The Indian sages were disturbed at them. They found a decline and fall of human civilization by such violations of human rights. The basic values of human existence—human essence—human personality as they conceived them—man's integrity, his freedom, his worth and value as an individual—were subjected to increasing restraint by the powerful. Certainly, they were human rights violations and the sages spoke against them by revealing the inspired truths. Those truths were seen in the mystical revelations. The revealed truths survived for centuries and the Indians still preserve them as sacred. Indians found that the ideas contained in the mystical teachings have been good—good to establish the human rights of all human beings on earth. This is what the United Nations are trying at present. The chapters that follow bring out the parallels on human rights and police as they are seen in Indian mystical teachings and in the U.N.'s Conventions and Declarations.

2

U.D.H.R., Police and Indian Mysticism

At the outset, one is confronted by an argument: "How could the mystics in India speak about police, human rights and United Nations?" People who raise such questions do not seem to be aware of the fact that human intellect is subordinate to intuition, divine inspiration and revelation from above. Human rights and the principles that guide human rights are not the results of academic abstractions, but are the foundations on which men exist and survive. The mystics make an outer expression to their inward realization—a kind of life experience. They get an insight into the nature of reality (*Darsana*) or experience the reality itself (*Anubhava*). This experience reveals eternal realities and human rights and their principles existed from the birth of man. It being so, the mystics experienced them much before human intellect could see them. It may be reiterated that the police is a new concept and the United Nations may be a still later organization. For a mystic, they could never be new. The mystics have a *vision of the soul.*

> "Oh men, direct your energies
> to promote the good of all
> mankind. Let your relations
> with all be characterized
> by love, peace and harmony.
> Let your hearts beat in
> Union with human hearts"

This is what is seen in *Ṛg Veda* (8, 49, 4). This is nothing but human rights and respect to human dignity. For, this insight is the radiant vision of the Divine expressed through the mystics. The mystic is gifted with a universality of outlook and that is the precise reason one argues that everything seen in today's world has some mystical foundations.

As said earlier, police—the word as such—is not seen in Indian mysticism. For, the word is of a later origin. But, the mystics could see police in their intuitive vision and could reveal the revealed truths. The truth could come out from them in strange tongues. When *ṛsis* or *seers* speak about power or authority, they talk about the police. They may not be telling that the police must be human rights friendly as the United Nations say in these days. At the same time, one may read in *Rg Veda* (4, 54, 3) "Whatever offence we have committed against the heavenly host, through feebleness of understanding or through pride or through human nature, O God, take from us this sin". This is a prayer which every offender has in his mind. He prays for mercy and forgiveness and the justice system functions as the God in such instances. "O Varuna, whatever the offence, which, we as men commit against the gods, whatever law of thine we may through ignorance violate punish us not, O God, for that iniquity" (*Ṛg Veda*, 7, 89). Again in *Atharva Veda* (4, 16, 1, 5) it is seen: "Absolve us from the sins of our fathers and from those which we have committed with our own bodies."

The police, as the law enforcement agency, have to take into account the mental state of a sinner—an offender in law and precisely, therefore, they have to be considerate and human rights friendly. United Nations, in the Universal Declaration of Human Rights have given due consideration to the state of mind of the offenders in law and have enacted several articles by virtue of which the police might deal with offenders in law. The United Nations want the police to be pure in their mind when they interact with offenders.

"Let thy mind be pure" (*Yajur Veda* 6,15). The police, it has been noted, down the centuries, behaving in a human rights unfriendly way to offenders under law. The United Nations wanted to give guidance to law enforcement machinery to be more human, just and honest to offenders under law.

> "May we throw off the
> interior impurities in the
> stream of knowledge and
> the exterior ones in that
> of water and thus we may
> become pure, fit for
> admittance into heaven" (*Atharva Veda* 14, 2, 67)

Universal Declaration of Human Rights (UDHR) and Police

Universal Declaration of Human Rights was not enacted for the police; nor was the Indian mysticism. But both are intended to guide the humanity. In the Preamble of the U.D.H.R. the intention was specified and it was to promote the development of "friendly relations" among the people and the mystics were giving inspired truths for the development of "human relations" among the people. "No friend is he who offers nothing to his friend and comrade" (*Ṛg Veda* 10, 117, 4). In *Atharva Veda* (19, 62, 1), it is revealed: 'O Lord, God Almighty, Grant me such qualities of head and heart, as would endear me to the enlightened and the learned among us, to the ruling class and to all men without distinction whether agriculturist and trader or artisan and labourer". In *Yajur Veda* (36, 18), it is reiterated: "Oh Lord, May I behold all the beings with the eye of a friend and may all the beings view me with kindly looks. May we look at each other with the eye of a friend.

> "Let our friendship be sincere with our brethren"
> (*Ṛg Veda* 4, 10, 8).

What noble thoughts! The United Nations in close scrutiny have just put down all these noble thoughts in the U.D.H.R. and they said:

> "All human beings are born free and equal in dignity. They are endowed with reason and conscience and should act towards one another in a spirit of brotherhood"
>
> (Article 1, U.D.H.R.).

During the British past, the Indian police were not exposed to such ideas which were seen in Indian mysticism. Even after India's independence, the police were not told about the Vedic revelations—and also the world views as seen in U.D.H.R. The world views which are held at high esteem in the international fora are seen in the *Vedas* of Hinduism, in the *Sutras* of Buddhism and in the teachings of Jainism.

Both the mystics and the United Nations emphasized the *"essence of man"*. Every man is a human being in essence and, therefore, everyone is born with dignity.

> "May I love everyone,
> whether noble or ignoble" (*Atharva Veda* 19, 26)

> "Those who malign
> Others are themselves maligned" (*Ṛg Veda,* 5, 2, 120)

> "Oh men, just as My commandments
> are for the whole mankind—for human
> beings, may be Brahmins,
> Kshatrias, Vaisyas,
> Shudras or even still low born people"
>
> (*Yajur Veda* 26, 2)

Infact, the Vedas of Hinduism is ahead of the U.N. vision. They speak more than what the U.N. speak on human dignity, equal rights and human essence. "Those who malign others are themselves maligned" and it means that those who do not respect man and his rights are themselves maligned. A human being—be he a violater of law or an observer of law—has human "*essence*". As such everyone has a *"manness"* in him. A rapist or a recidivist in this sense has a *human essence* and precisely, therefore, he is equal in dignity with other human beings who are law abiding.

Indian scriptures, saints and sages have, respectfully and repeatedly, reiterated the worth of human person—human essence time and again—centuries before the United Nations were formed.

"He attains excellence who looks with equal regard upon well wishers, friends, foes, neutrals and arbiters, upon the hateful, the relatives and upon the righteous and unrighteous alike" (*Gita*). Human essence is respected here not only among the friends and well wishers but also among the foes, the hateful and unrighteous. Policemen who read the scriptures will certainly try to see human essence in everyone—in the suspect, in the victim, in the witness, in the complainant, in the politician, in the affluent and so on.

Look into *Bhavishya Purana* and see that the thoughts are superior to the thoughts of U.N. in U.D.H.R. For, one sees: "As if there be four sons of a person and the caste of all those four is one and the same, so is the whole creation the offspring of one heavenly father and being the children of the same father, there is no difference of their caste or race". The human essence is more respected here. Everyone is regarded as the offspring of one heavenly father. All are treated as the children of the same father and there is no difference among various castes and races.

What more does one need to accept the fact that every man has the same *human essence?* "I am the same in all the beings, neither is any dearer to Me or hateful. They who serve Me with devotion are contained in Me and I in them" (*Gita*, 9, 21). This is human essence and as such there is no difference between the world view expressed by the United Nations and the same by Hinduism—*i.e.*, All human beings are born free and equal in dignity and rights" (U.D.H.R.) Since the man has "*human essence*", idiots, saints, lepers, crime-doers and law abiding citizens have equal rights and dignity. Throughout the history of mankind, the criminals are not respected and they are approached with a retributive spirit. Sometimes, they are humiliated, harassed, victimized and tortured by people including the police. It was indeed difficult for people to think that the murderers, the rapists, the thieves, the burglars, sex offenders—all of them had equal dignity. Today, the objective of punishment has been recognized as correction and rehabilitation of the offenders and as such the world view of the United Nations and the mystical views of the Indian *ṛsis* assume equal importance.

> "A man is not just, if he carries a matter by violence"
> (*Dhammapada*, 19)

> "God protects him who is just and
> truthful and destroys him who is not so"
> (*Ṛg Veda* 7, 104, 12)

> "The heaven and earth sustain a justice loving man"
> (*Ṛg Veda* 3, 26, 9)

> "Justice without generosity may easily become Shylock's justice" (Gandhiji).

The United Nations too have said nothing more than what we read in our scriptures and in the writings of great men.

The Universal Declaration of Human Rights contains articles intended to protect the interest of the suspects, accused and crime doers.

Article 3 (U.D.H.R.)
"Everyone has the right to life, liberty and security of person"

Article 4 (U.D.H.R.)
"No one shall be subjected to torture or to cruel, inhuman or degrading treatment or punishment"

Article 6 (U.D.H.R.)
"Everyone has the right to recognition everywhere as a person before the law".

What is the meaning of human essence and existence if he does not possess a right to his life? Yet, one listens to custodial deaths, suicides and murders and they happen during the course of law enforcement! It means that an agency instituted to protect the life of people becomes an agency responsible for causing death! The protector, as stated elsewhere becomes the annihilator and certainly it is a human rights violation. No man is the creator of his body and no man has the right to put an end to his life. If that is so, how can another put an end to another man's life?

> "Our Father, Our Creator,
> Our Disposer, Who knows
> all positions, all things
> existing" (*Ṛg Veda* 10, 82, 3)

and He only has the right to take away the life of a man which he has entrusted to his responsible care and concern. In *Atharva Veda* (2, 1, 3), one reads:

> "He is our Father
> Our Progenitor,
> Our Friend"

and if that is so, it is not only the human rights of people to have his life protected, but also it is a divine commandment.

> "God is our friend,
> Our Father,
> And our Supporter
> And Protector (*Yajur Veda* 32, 10)

How can the law enforcement agency cause custodial death? United Nations do not favour the infliction of capital punishment to the convicted. They say it in their resolutions against death penalty:

"Affirms that, in order fully to guarantee the right to life, provided for in Article 3 of the Universal Declaration of Human Rights, the main objective to be pursued is that of progressively restricting the number of offences for which capital punishment may be imposed, with a view to the desirability of abolishing this punishment in all countries". (2027th plenary meeting 20 December, 1971). Any number of passages can be found in Indian scriptures respecting human life and recognizing *the right to live* as a human right.

> "He is within our own hearts
> He has lodged Himself in
> the food—stained body of
> man and rules both body
> and life, even He that
> sustains the whole universe
> and all its glory" (*Mundaka Upanishad*, 11, 2, 7)

and if that is the truth, *He* alone has the right to annihilate a human being—and no one else. "Concentrating the mind on the spirit within, man should realise the divine character of his own soul and its inherent freedom" (*Katha Upanishad* 2, 18). Thus, Indian scriptures accepted the inherent freedom of the human soul long before the world community thought about it. U.D.H.R. (Article 3) makes it a human right to have the freedom of man—*i.e.,* liberty. It means that the police do not have any authority to effect illegal arrests or detention of people who are taken into custody. But, allegations are there that the police do so during law enforcement and crime investigation. Certainly, it is a human rights violation and the world community is against such objectionable practices, if they exist. What did the mystics and the holy sages in India speak about human freedom/liberty. *Ṛsis* and Indian sages accepted human freedom.

"There are two ways—one of the worldly pleasure and the other of bliss. Of the two, those *who take up the good* are blessed while those *who take to evil,* do not attain success" (*Katha Upanishad* 1, 2, 1) It means that the freedom of man was a reality for them. "Right to liberty"—was accepted in Indian Constitution as a fundamental right. Courts of law protect this right. Human rights law upholds this right as sacred. Nevertheless, there exists some controversies on this point between United Nations and Indian Mysticism.

Controversies between United Nations and Current Criminological Thoughts

Police deal with people including criminals. The fundamental question is: "can the police consider that all human beings are born free and equal in dignity and rights?". Sociologists may argue that every child is born into a family—into a community—into a society—into a country and culture. Certainly, he is tied up by many forces which are beyond his control. Police deal with people who are born and brought up in a family, community, culture etc. Cesare Lombroso said that a criminal was born. Bentham and Beccaria brought pleasure and pain to explain criminal behaviour. They said that men had free-will. Psychologists explained criminal behaviour on the basis of personality factors, mental disorders, impact of *unconscious, id complexes* etc...Endocrinologists brought out endocrine malfunctionings. There was multiple causation approach. The policemen became at their wit's end and, therefore, they were more concerned with what did the criminal do than why did the criminal commit a particular crime.

Policemen accepted the fact that every man has human *essence,* but some of them believed that they did not have *human existence.* They argued that there was difference between essence and existence. They felt that all human beings (having human essence) did not have *human existence.* A rapist, a murderer, a cheat—all of them had human *essence,* but they did not have human *existence.* They thought that all human beings were equal in dignity as far as their essence was concerned. But, they were unequal as far as the human existence was concerned. A criminal, some police officers said, had the essence of a man and the existence of a crime-doer.

Dignity in Random College Dictionary means *nobility.* What is the dignity (nobility) of a cheat? of a terrorist? of a rapist? of a murderer? If the policemen give respect to a rapist as he gives respect to the raped, it shows wrong signals. If rapists, smugglers, cheats, thieves etc. are respected just like saints and sages, then what will be the social response to such police behaviour? Throughout the history of mankind, the criminals are not respected. For, respecting criminals means respecting crimes and encouraging criminal behaviour. Human rights activists and United Nations insist that all human beings including criminals must be respected. Police ask: "to the essence of a criminal or to the existence of a criminal". Indian philosophy says: "Man is composed of soul and body. The body is perishable, the soul is immortal and eternal. It is *Brahman* itself. In the *Upanishads*, there are passages: *"that thou are* (*tat tvam asi*) and *"I am Brahman"*. These passages speak only the essence of man and not all the existence of man. The soul of every individual exists within the individual. What are the rights of a criminal who has human essence and criminal existence? Criminals have all the rights guaranteed by the laws and therefore they must be dealt with as per the law and the procedure established by law. Different countries have different procedures and laws. Policemen say that: "so long as there exist no International Penal Code, Code of Criminal Procedure, Evidence Act etc., it is virtually not possible to say the rights of a suspect, of an accused, of a crime-doer—in specific terms—in international terms". Indian mysticism has many concepts which can be the guiding principles of man throughout the world.

Police and Torture

United Nations have a Convention called "Convention Against Torture and Other Cruel, Inhuman or Degrading Treatment or Punishment" and the same is discussed at length in a separate chapter. Torture is the result of no reverence to fellow human beings and, therefore, it is a violation of human rights. U.N. condemns torture on any human beings including criminals. Parallels to U.N. thinkings may be seen in Indian mysticism.

> "Reverence to the great ones,
> Reverence to the lesser ones,
> Reverence to the young,
> Reverence to the old (*Ṛg Veda* 1, 27, 13)

and lack of reverence to human person means employment of torture, degrading treatment, cruel and inhuman approaches. The mystics did not approve of such barbarous acts.

Human rights and torture by police are interlinked by some human rights activists. Why do the police become aggressive to people? Police know that employment of torture is a human rights violation, yet they are involved in it. Is it not true?

"Let a man overcome anger by kindness, evil by good"—Buddha said so and his teachings could be taken by all law enforcement agencies including the police. Anger, no doubt, is a cause of using torture on people. The one who employs torture and the one who receives torture—both have human rights. Cicero once said:

> "Anger is to be very specially avoided in inflicting punishment"

and law enforcement officers must bear this in mind. More about torture and mystical thinkings is discussed elsewhere in this book. Hindu mystical revelations are concerned with timeless truths which guide the people to eternity. The relation of mystical knowledge to human rights is just one of its many aspects.

"Everyone has the right to recognition everywhere as a person before law"—the United Nations categorically proclaimed so in their U.D.H.R. in 1948. But, centuries ago, the mystics said that:

> "For one who lives according to Eternal law, the winds are full of sweetness; the rivers pour sweetness; so may plants be full of sweetness for us. Sweet be the night and sweet the dawns, sweet the dust of the earth, sweet be our Father in Heaven to us. For us may the forests be full of sweetness, full of sweetness the sun, and full of sweetness the kine for us" (*Ṛg Veda* 1, 90).

Everyone is recognized as a person before the Eternal laws and the man-made laws are just the reflections of the *Eternal laws.* Everyone who lives according to *Eternal laws* are recognized and there is no distinction among them in so far as they receive the sweetness. In *Gita,* it is seen: "The Lord dwelleth in the hearts of all beings (*Gita* XVIII, 61) and there is no discrimination here. Everybody is recognized as a person—a person with dignity and that is the reason why it is stated in *Gita* that the "Lord dwelleth in the hearts of all beings".

> "They verily who worship Me
> with devotion, they are in
> Me and I also in them" (*Gita* IX, 29)

and it means that everybody is recognized by God as equal to anybody. God lives in everyone and what more recognition one needs?

> "Who is sinless in mind, without jealousy, calm, pure in action, the friend of all whose words are pleasant and profitable, devoid of pride and fraud, the Lord always dwells in his heart" (*Vishnu Purana II*, 7, 23)

What is the law after all? The law is God and the God is the law. He treats everyone equal before Him and He recognizes everyone as a human being—with human essence, worth and dignity. The United Nations have just reiterated this mystic concept in their own words and made an article under U.D.H.R. *Ṛg Veda* (2, 27, 14) reads: "May not the lord of darkness come over us" and it comes over those who do not recognize and respect human rights.

Police in India have been concerned only with the penal, procedural and evidence laws and have never been informed of mystical teachings and human rights laws. The impact has been that they did have a number of *guiding principles,* but did not know much about the *guided principles.* The mystical revelations show the *guided principles* as well as the *guiding principles* so much so that they become laws for eternity. Police are blamed to use torture and if it is true, why do they use it? They do not give due respect to the guiding principles and the principles which guide the guiding principles. The central aim of Indian mysticism is to teach humanity about the guiding and guided principles—and these principles come from an ultimate reality. Hindus call it *Brahman.*

"May we get from the gods
that wisdom which works
for the good" (*Ṛg Veda* 1, 89, 2)

"May the blissful love of the
righteous gods be ours, the
grace of gods lie about us" (*Ṛg Veda* 1, 89, 2)

and the human rights laws proclaimed by United Nations are just the extension of what the mystics in India revealed long-long ago. Police if they accept the mystical revelations, necessarily they have to be human rights friendly. The human rights laws of the United Nations are not an accidental product of that organization. They have their roots in mystical revelations and teachings and one of the reasons why the police in India could not/did not become people friendly in the past—even today—is due to their lack of knowledge in the revealed truths of Indian sages and *ṛsis*.

3

United Nations, Unity of Purpose, Police and Mysticism

"Numerous thin threads of equal length collected are competent to bear, from strength of numbers, the constant rolling of the shuttlecock over him. The case is even so with relatives that are good. Separate from one another, burning brands produce only smoke, but brought together they blaze forth into a powerful flame. And a tree that stands single, though gigantic and strong and deep rooted, hath its trunk soon smashed and twisted by almighty wind. Those trees, however, that stand erect, growing close together, are competent to resist winds more violent still, owing to mutual dependence. Thus, he that is single, however endowed with all the virtues, is regarded by foes as capable of being vanquished like an isolated tree by the wind (*Mahabharata, Udyoga Parva*, Sec. 36). The United Nations want international co-operation and willing participation of member-States to see that human rights are respected everywhere alike.

"Remember, there can be no happiness for anyone unless it is won for all (Sir Jagadish Chandra Bose) and that is the precise reason why the United Nations insist and pressure all nations to recognize human rights—*All rights for all.* For, man has equal rights everywhere in the world. The rights are inalienable, eternal and universal. The world community knows that "it is with united effort that good deeds can be done" (*Atharva Veda* 20, 128, 12) and that is, perhaps, the only reason why the Universal Declaration of Human Rights was proclaimed as soon as the United Nations was formed.

U.D.H.R. and Police

> "No one shall be subjected to arbitrary arrest, detention or exile" (Article 9, U.D.H.R.)

"No one shall be subjected to arbitrary interference with his privacy, family, home or correspondence, nor to attacks upon his honour and reputation. Everyone has the right to the protection of the law against such interference or attacks" (Article 12, U.D.H.R.). These are two articles which are connected to police. "Arbitrary" means "subject to individual will or judgement without restriction—contingent solely upon one's discretion" (The Random House College Dictionary). The police are accused of having recourse to arbitrary arrests of people for many things and anything. About the arrests by police and the need to arrest people, the National Police Commission had made unfavourable comments and they found that many arrests were unnecessary. The news relating to such arbitrary arrests may appear in the media. The Supreme Court of India issued directives to be followed when arrests are made. Probably, arbitrary arrests by police may be an international phenomenon so much so that the United Nations prohibit the same. It is stated in the Universal Declaration of Human Rights. The observations of police commissions, research workers, media, Supreme Court etc... on arrests, unnecessary arrests and arbitrary arrests are instructions to police on what to do or what not to do. The United Nations too do the same and all of them teach duties—duties and duties to be performed in a human rights friendly way.

"After having taught the *Vedas*, the teacher instructs the pupil thus: "Speak what is true. Do your duties" (*Taittriya Upanishad,* 1,1). The United Nations too do the same thing with a hope that the human rights friendly States will do their duties in the way desired by the world community. They are not expected to neglect their duties.

> "They who neglect their social duties for their individual life fall in darkness and those who sacrifice their individuality for social popularity fall into greater darkness" (*Isha Upanishad*).

There is an allegation that some people are arbitrarily arrested and some people are not arrested by police—even with convincing evidence. Why? There is human rights violation here and any discrimination made between man and man, man and woman in this area is treated as human rights unfriendly.

"He who is a (faithful and true) servant of the Lord is like the Lord himself. Make no distinction between man and man just like the ripples of water which rise in water and get absorbed in it" (Gauri Kabir). Who has got the powers to arrest a citizen in an arbitrary way? The Indian *risis* did not or could not see the arrests which the police effect now in an arbitrary way; nevertheless they said that everyone ought to be duty conscious. A man conscious of his duties could not think of arbitrary arrests.

What are the duties and responsibilities of a police officer to their detinues? Here too, the United Nations speak about arbitrary detention and they prohibit the same at any cost. What purpose does such detention serve to humanity?

United Nations have brought out a body of principles for the Protection of All Persons under Any Form of Detention or Imprisonment"—(General Assembly Resolution 43/173). In that they state that a detained person means "any person deprived of personal liberty except as a result of conviction for an offence" and they continue that a detained person must be "treated in a humane manner and with respect for the inherent dignity of the human person". Indian mysticism goes a step further and states that all persons must be treated in a humane manner.

"He who serves and pleases people with his eyes, mind, speech and deeds attains higher regions" (*Mahabharata*) and it contains everything contained in the words "in a humane manner".

"What reward does one get by rendering services? By service, one attains nearness of God" (*Uttradhain Sutra*, 29, 43). Police is a service and rendering police service in a human rights friendly way makes the service meaningful and praiseworthy. Policemen are accused of employing filthy expressions to the detinues in their custody and certainly, it is a human right violation.

> "A person of good acts and good, agreeable and sweet speech has no equal" (*Mahabharata, Santi Parva*, 84, 10).

> "One should have cool temper and should never utter

unpleasant words" (*Uttradhain Sutra,* 1, 8).

What do the United Nations speak to the police? They say that the police must be humane to people. They must not be inhuman, barbarous and animal like when they interact with people. In the case of detinues, the United Nations lay down:

> "No person under any form of detention or imprisonment shall be subjected to torture or to cruel, inhuman or degrading treatment or punishment. No circumstance whatever may be invoked as a justification for torture or other inhuman or degrading treatment or punishment".

The United Nations give a further clarification here:

> "The term *cruel, inhuman or degrading* treatment or punishment should be interpreted so as to extend the widest possible protection against abuses, whether physical or mental including the holding of a detained or imprisoned person in conditions which deprive him, temporarily or permanently, of the use of any of his natural senses, such as sight or hearing, or of his awareness of place and the passing of time".

In a nutshell, the United Nations insist that all people detained by an authority must be treated with decency, dignity, honour and humaneness. Indian spiritualism says that such treatment must be offered to all people.

"He who beareth no ill will to any being, friendly and compassionate, without attachment and egoism, balanced in pleasure and pain and forgiving, ever content, harmonious with the self controlled resolute mind and reason dedicated to Me; he, my devotee, is dear to Me" (*Gita* XII, 13,14). "To any being"—that is what is written in *Gita* and the detinue is included there. The Indian mystical teachings are always in favour of kindness, compassion, friendliness to other fellow human beings.

"Let a man overcome anger by kindness, evil by good"
(The Buddha)

"The Lord dwelleth in the hearts of all beings"
(*Gita,* XVIII, 61).

Why must the police or people in authority behave in a cruel way to the detinues? The main reason may be that they do not understand the worth of human person and dignity. They lack purity of intentions.

"Serenity of mind, kindliness, silence, self-control, honesty of motive—this is called the austerity of mind" (*Gita* XVII, 16). Certainly, every law enforcement officer must have the honesty of motive. United Nations further say:

> "It shall be prohibited to take undue advantage of the situation of a detained or imprisoned person for the purpose of compelling him to confess, to incriminate himself otherwise or to testify against any other person.
> No detained person while being interrogated shall be subject to violence, threats or methods of interrogation which impair his capacity of decision or his judgement" (Principle 21, Body of Principles for the Protection of All Persons under Any Form of Detention or Imprisonment, United Nations).

Indian mysticism is totally against violence of any kind. The United Nations have just accepted it and incorporated it in the principle proclaimed for detainees. Gandhiji said: "violence is suicide". What do the police achieve in becoming violent to a detinue in their custody? "When a man hurts you, and you turn back to hurt him that would not cure the first injury; it would only create in the world one more wickedness" (Buddha) and torturing a detinue is not law enforcement, but is lawless law enforcement. "Here in this world, anger is never pacified by anger. By non-anger is anger pacified. This is the ancient law" (*Dhammapada*, 1, 5). This is the reason why Gandhiji forcefully said: "The way of non-violence and truth is as sharp as a razor's edge". This is Indian thought and necessarily, it is the principle to be followed by police during crime investigation as well. How must the police collect evidence against a suspect? They must collect the evidence not through violent means, but by employing psychological means and scientific methods. "As a humble bee extracts essence from all kinds of flowers, likewise a wise man collecteth essence from all scriptures" (*Bhagvata Purana*, 11, 8, 17). Similarly, a police investigator must gather information and collect evidence from the suspects during interrogation or otherwise. This is the reason why

United Nations insist:

> "No detained or imprisoned person shall even with his consent, be subjected to any medical or scientific experimentation which may be detrimental to his health" (Principle 22, Body of Principles for the Protection of All Persons under Any Form of Detention or Imprisonment, United Nations).

Human Rights and Privacy

Right to privacy is a sacred human right and any interference with family, home etc., is prohibited by the world community. 'Family' is a sacred place honoured by Indian culture. Police, while they conduct a raid in a house, must respect the dignity of the women inside.

> "Where women are honoured, gods are happy. Where women are not respected, all efforts come to naught" (Manu).

The police must bear this in mind so that no allegation of indecency and gender indignity is raised against the police. How to deal with women during a raid in a house or when women are interacted? The Buddha advises:

> "Guard yourself against looking on a woman. If you see a woman, let it be as though you saw her not, and have no conversation with her. If, after all, you must speak with her, let it be with a pure heart and think to yourself 'I' as a *shramana*, will live in this sinful world as a spotless leaf of the lotus, unsoiled by the mud in which it grows. If the woman be old, regard her as your mother; if young, as your sister; if very young, as your child. The *shramana* who looks at a woman as a woman or touches her as a woman has broken the vow and is no longer the disciple of the Sakyamuni.... Lust beclouds a man's heart when it is confused with woman's beauty and the mind is dazed. Better far with hot irons lore out both your eyes than encourage in yourselves sensual thoughts, or look upon a woman's form

> with lustful desires. Better fall into the fierce tiger's mouth or under the sharp knife of the executioner, than to dwell with a woman and excite in yourself lustful thoughts.... Therefore, I say restrain the heart, give it no bridle licence".

How many policemen/officers will be able to look at a woman as advised by Buddha? If they do so, there will not be any question of any custodial molestation or custodial rape as alleged against the policemen during law enforcement or crime investigation. Chanakya says: "He who looks upon all women as his own mother.. is a truly learned man" and this must be the attitude and approach of policemen/officers to women.

Arbitrary interference with the privacy of a man/woman is a forbidden act under human rights law. Every man/woman has privacies and one should not interfere with it. Those who do not honour the privacies of others are not keeping decorum and self esteem.

> "Observe decorum, if good name you seek;
> If nobleness, before the great be meek" (Tirukkural)

and Tagore reminds: "Civility is a beauty of behaviour". Those who do not show respect to others' privacies are not expressing civility. Policemen claim that they are a very disciplined lot and then human rights activists ask: "How can the police interfere with the privacies of others?". The police conduct surveillance and shadowing of suspects. The Supreme Court of India has given certain directives to police as to how they must conduct surveillance and shadowing of suspects in a human rights friendly way—keeping dignity and decorum. The policemen, if they claim to be disciplined, must keep away from interfering with the privacies of others.

"Ignorance and absence of discipline are the cause of man's troubles" (Kautilya) and can we say that the troubles with police is that they are not disciplined well?

Never attack upon one's honour and reputation. This is a human right law. Instances are plenty to show that police officers/men handcuff people unnecessarily—just to humiliate them—just to demoralize them. Sometimes, photographs of the arrestees with no shirt on their bodies appear in the press. Photographs of pickpockets are exhibited in railway stations, bus stands, police exhibition stalls etc. This may be of bad taste and is not approved by people. Detinues are detained in nakedness/half-nakedness in police lock-ups and if the allegation is true, the attitude is blameworthy. Policemen/officers are blamed to use filthy expressions/epithets calculated to attack upon the honour and reputation of the people who listen to such undesirable comments, words etc. The fact that an individual has committed an offence, does not mean that he loses all his respect and he cannot enjoy human rights. Who is a saint in police service? Violation of human rights itself is a crime and whenever a policeman attacks the honour and reputation of others—including crime-doers—he commits a crime.

"There is no one in the world who is not blamed"—says the Buddha. All men commit crimes—not always. "There never was, there never will be, nor is there now, a man who is always blamed, or a man who is always praised" (*Dhammapada* 17) Anything the police may do will not receive due acceptance if they do not show respect to the honour and reputation of others.

"Even gifts, if not made with agreeable speeches, do not delight the recipients, like rice without curry.

If even the possessions of men be taken away with sweet speeches, such sweetness of behaviour succeeds in reconciling the robbed" (*Mahabharata, Shanti Parva* 84, 5-8). Hence, the police must have a grace when they enforce laws.

"May we get from the gods that wisdom which works for the good" (*Ṛg Veda*, 1, 89, 2). If the police do not respect others, it means that they are showing disrespect to them and to the law they enforce.

"It is He who inspires to do good works, the man whom He will lead on high, and it is He who inspires to do evil works, the man whom He will lead downwards" (*Mundaka Upanishad* III, 2, 3). Any police work which does not exhibit respect to others and decorum to the uniform they wear will lead them downwards. Police must know the worth and value of police work. Those who do not respect the value and worth of police work are in ignorance and they will be bad models for all others who enforce law.

"As people ignorant of the presence of a golden treasure which has been hidden underground, may walk over it again and again and yet never find it, so all beings though every moment living in *Brahman* never find Him for He is hidden by a layer of ignorance" (*Chandogya Upanishad* VIII, 3, 2). This is what is happening in the case of some police officers who perform their duties without respecting *Brahman* in others.

Judgement on Others

The police have to make several decisions, but are not expected to make judgements on others. The Universal Declaration of Human Rights reads: "Everyone is entitled in full equality to a fair and public hearing by an independent and impartial tribunal, in the determination of his rights and obligations and of any criminal charge against him" (Article 10, U.D.H.R.). The police must not sit on judgement. Let it be done by an impartial judiciary. The police see only one side, the prosecution and an impartial judiciary sees both sides—the prosecution and defence. The decision of an impartial judiciary will be balanced and fair.

> "They place good and evil deeds in a balance whichever of the two shall outweigh the other, that he shall follow, whether it is good or evil.... it is by good deeds and not by bad, that his scale outweighs"
>
> (*Satapatha Brahmana* XI, 2, 7, 33).

Indian mysticism, United Nations, the world community—all speak the same thing in different or same language. All are concerned with the urgency of enforcing human rights for the social development. All affirm the inadequacies in the attention paid to human rights violations. All are aware of the bad deeds people commit and all know the evil effects and the ramification of such evil deeds if not checked in time. They teach us and seldom we listen to them. The sacred scriptures said these things long back—and the United Nations said them in the recent past—and the world community accepts them now. The United Nations request the Secretary General to take appropriate steps to enforce human rights laws—to strengthen the U.N. activities for promoting the same. The United Nations invite all governments to make continuous efforts to implement the world accepted human rights laws always and everywhere.

4

International Covenants, Human Rights and Indian Mysticism

"One should never do that to another which one regards as injurious to one's own self. This, in brief, is the rule of righteousness" (*Anushasana Parva*, 1113, 8). But, one sees the denial of equal rights to another because of caste, skin, colour, sex, origin and what not? Discrimination is a violation of human rights and there must be united efforts to remove such discriminatory treatment. "It is with united effort that good deeds can be done" (*Atharva Veda* 20, 128-12). It being so, the nations in the world united themselves and proclaimed two international covenants for enforcing human rights. They are—

1. International Covenant on Economic, Social and Cultural Rights [Adopted and opened for signature, ratification and accession by General Assembly Resolution 2200 A(XXI) of 16 December, 1966. Entry into force on 3 January, 1976, in accordance with Article 27].
2. International Covenant on Civil and Political Rights (Adopted and opened for signature, ratification and accession by General Assembly, December, 1966. Entry into force on 23 March, 1976, in accordance with Article 49).

The second Covenant contains some articles which have direct or indirect bearing on police and police functioning and United Nations want international acceptance, co-operation and assistance to achieve the objective. To quote from the Preamble—

> "Considering the obligation of States under the Charter of the United Nations to promote universal respect for and observance of human rights and freedom.
> "Realizing that the individual, having duties to other individuals and to the community to which he belongs, is under a responsibility to strive for the promotion and observance of the rights recognized in the present Covenant.
> "Agree upon the following articles".

The articles which have bearing on police and the ideas conveyed through such articles were already accepted and seen in Indian mystical revelations.

"Every human being has the inherent right to life" (Article 6, ICCPR). Man must have this right, for "man is the perfection of the creations" (*Chandogya Upanishad* 2, 6, 1). How can a man be denied of his inherent right to live? Indian mystics say that God is the creator of man and he alone can take away the life of man.

> "He is our Father, our
> Progenitor, our Friend" (*Atharva Veda,* 2, 1, 3)

> "Our Father, our Creator,
> our Deposer, who knows
> all positions, all things existing" (*Ṛg Veda* 10, 82, 3)

It being so, no one has any authority to deny the inherent right to life. In *Svetasvatara Upanishad* (VI, 16-17), it is written—

> "He is the maker of all, the all-knower, self-sourced, intelligent, the author of time, possessor of qualities, omniscient, is the ruler of primary matter and of the spirit, the Lord of qualities...consisting of that immortal existing as the Lord, intelligent, omnipresent, the guardian of this world, is He who constantly rules this world. There is no other cause found for ruling".

This entire mysticism speaks only on the worth of human life and makes God as the creator. In such a background, United Nations' view that every man has an inherent right to life is only a tautology about which the mystics have already said in the past.

From the police-angle, this article assumes a lot of importance as the news about custodial death in police is not rare. There is an allegation that people die in police custody all over the world and there is a conscious attempt everywhere to make such deaths as suicidal deaths. This happens in the west, east, north and south and the United Nations make it known to people and nations that custodial death is a heinous crime and a human rights violation. India is a signatory to the above Covenant and, therefore, death in police custody is treated now as a human rights violation. Compensation is awarded by Human Rights Commissions in case custodial murder takes place in police department.

'Inherent' means 'existing in something as a permanent and inseparable element, quality or attribute' (The Random House College Dictionary) and United Nations recently and Indian mystics in ancient times said so—said in such a way that the right to life is an inviolable (secure from destruction, violence, infringement or desecration) right which is inalienable (not alienated; not transferable to another or capable of being repudiated) to people. It is a birth right and it can be terminated only in a natural way—through a natural course. The Indian mysticism accepted man's right to life. Dr. S. Radhakrishnan writes: "To look upon life as an evil and treat the world as a delusion is sheer ingratitude". Whatever that be, no police officer/man has any authority to do anything with the life of a man whatever may be the objectives. Human rights law of the United Nations says that the right to life "shall be protected by law. No one shall be arbitrarily deprived of his life".

The United Nations continue: "In countries which have not abolished the death penalty, sentence of death may be imposed only for the most serious crimes in accordance with the law in force at the time of the commission of the crime and not contrary to the provisions of the present Covenant and to the Convention on the Prevention and Punishment of the Crime of Genocide. This penalty can only be carried out pursuant to a final judgement rendered by a competent court". [Article 6(2) ICCPR]. Death penalty is disfavoured for criminals. Indian sages fully agree in their opinion on this issue. One may see that India still awards capital punishment in rarest of rare cases. Death penalty does not offer any chance for the crime-doers for repentance. Today, criminologists and penologists accept correction and repentance.

> "Absolve us from the sins
> of our fathers and from
> those which we have committed
> with our own bodies" (*Atharva Veda* 4, 16, 1, 5).

Indian mystic revelations were thus in favour of offering opportunities for sinners (crime-doers) to repent over their evil doings.

> "May the gods who are all knowing, the lords of everything, animate and inanimate, help us to go beyond our sins, committed and uncommitted (*i.e.*, present and future) for our ultimate good" (*Ṛg Veda* 63, 8).

"Whatever offence we have committed against the heavenly host, through feebleness of understanding or through pride, or through human nature, O God, take from us this sin" (*Ṛg Veda*, 4, 54, 3). Thus, the most current view that the criminal does not lose his chance to repent over the crime just because he commits a crime is an accepted view in ancient India. Police are, now and then, accused of causing custodial death and there is no justification in what they do in the pretext of administering justice.

Article 7 of ICCPR reads:

> "No one shall be subjected to torture or to cruel, inhuman or degrading treatment or punishment. In particular, no one shall be subjected without his free consent to medical or scientific experimentation".

Somehow or other, people connect torture with police. They think that the police subject people to cruel, inhuman or degrading treatment. The allegations are not altogether baseless as there may be a number of cases of custodial torture reported and proved to be correct. In some cases, policemen/officers have been punished. It may be reiterated that Indian mysticism does not favour violence and torture.

"Frenzy has eighteen defects.....hatred of men, factitiousness, censoriousness, untruthful speech, lust, wrath, want of control, speaking ill of others, back-biting, mismanagement in business, quarrelsomeness, animosity, troubling living creatures, want of forgiveness, delusion, flippancy, loss of reason. Therefore, a wise man should not be the subject to frenzy, for it is always censured" (*Sanatsugatya* V). There is no scope for employing torture in police work and the Indian laws which were enacted as early as in 1860 (Indian Penal Code) were against the employment of torture by police. Indian Evidence Act 1872 and the Code of Criminal Procedure too favoured the same. Even before United Nations made the human rights law against torture, Indians implemented the principle in their laws. Perhaps, the mystical thoughts were, to some extent, inspiring the law-makers to do so. Tirukkural says: "To use harsh words when kind words are at hand is picking unripe fruit where ripe fruit hangs".

"Forbearance, forgiveness, self-control, non-stealing, purity, control of senses, virtuous intellect, knowledge, truthfulness, absence of anger are the ten laws of righteousness" (*Manu Smriti,* 6, 92). If this was the attitude of Indians, where could one find the place for torture?

"He, who under the influence of his evil propensities injures me or intends to injure me, is injured himself by his own wickedness and evil nature, then why should I retaliate?" (*Ṛg Veda,* 8, 18, 13). What a noble inspiration for policemen when they enforce law or investigate crimes. What could the police achieve so far by the use of third degree methods? Nothing—or, perhaps, ill-name and hatred. Police could not get an acceptance and recognition for the work they do, not even for the good service they render. To repeat the same that has been said earlier.

"Let a man overcome anger by kindness, evil by good"—The Buddha. If this thought can inspire the policemen, then human rights law against torture, cruel, inhuman or degrading treatment or punishment becomes meaningless and irrelevant.

Arrest, Detention and Human Rights

Article 9, ICCPR is about arrest, detention, compensation etc. and it reads:

"1. Everyone has the right to liberty and security of person. No one shall be subjected to arbitrary arrest or detention. No one shall be deprived of his liberty except on such grounds and in accordance with such procedure as are established by law.
2. Anyone who is arrested shall be informed, at the time of arrest, of the reasons for his arrest and shall be promptly informed of any charges against him."

Right to liberty and security of person is the most honoured right. Some human rights activists in the west still adhere to the view that the concept of freedom is their contribution to humanity. Rousseau said: "A country cannot subsist well without liberty, nor liberty without virtue". Pope Leo XIII stated: "The true liberty of human society does not consist in every man doing what he pleases, for this would simply end in turmoil and confusion, and bring on the overthrow of the State; but rather in this, that through the injunctions of the civil law all may more easily conform to the prescriptions of the eternal law". What are these eternal laws? Indian mystics had given these eternal laws long before the westerners thought about it. Pinchard once said: "True liberty consists in the privilege of enjoying our own rights, not in the destruction of the rights of others".

What is seen in Indian mystical revelations?

"Man winneth not freedom from action, by abstaining from activity, nor by mere renunciation doth he rise to perfection" (*Gita,* III, 4). Man has to work and he cannot be free if he does not do anything. He must enjoy freedom to do many things and everyone has the right to liberty, Freedom is not unlimited—unrestricted: There is the eternal law which restrains man from doing something or from exercising his freedom "He who ignoring the teachings of scriptures, acts according to his will, cannot attain success, nor happiness nor emancipation. Therefore, to determine what ought to be done and what ought not to be done, scripture is the authority" (*Gita* 18, 23, 24). Policemen, when they perform their duties, must be conscious of their duties—the duties being that (1) nobody shall be deprived of his liberty in an arbitrary way, (2) no torture, cruel or inhuman treatment to anybody and they must not have any place when dealing with the arrestees. For, such behaviour is against the eternal laws seen in Indian mysticism.

Everyone has the right to the security of person—says ICCPR and the inspired truths call them (people who commit anything against the security of others) evil doers. "The evil doers cannot cross the path of truth" (*Ṛg Veda* 9, 73, 6). Man's life and his security are precious and another man cannot and should not take away the rights of others. "God alone is the creator, protector and supporter of life" (*Yajur Veda* 32, 10) "God is known through His laws" (*Ṛg Veda* 1, 22, 9) and God's law does not permit people to do anything that affects adversely the life and security of other human beings.

The human rights law says that the arrestees have a right to know the time of arrest, reasons for the arrest etc., and they are nothing but the essential minimum requirement to be decent to people who are arrested. All throughout the mystical inspirations, one sees only decency and decorum in human behaviour. It goes without saying that one should be honestly neat and decent to the arrestees. The policemen who arrest the people ought to be decent and human rights friendly. They are to render service to people and humanity and the human rights laws are nothing but instructions as to how one must render human service to people keeping dignity and honour.

"Let my life be a life of dedication; let my vital breath, eyes, ears, intellect and spirit be dedicated to service; let my love and my understanding, my prosperity and my knowledge be dedicated to service. Let the service be made in a spirit of utter sacrifice" (*Upanishads*). What a noble inspiration indeed if policemen can listen to it! Police job is a mission—a vocation—a divine gift and it must be performed only in a spirit of service.

"Oh Lord, may we share
among ourselves the gifts
granted by Thee and lead
a peaceful life" (*Ṛg Veda*, 2, 13, 4).

Certainly a policeman who is human rights friendly will experience pleasure, peace and happiness in life. He can do so if and only if he performs his duties as per law and the procedure established by law. The human rights law insists that "anyone who has been a victim of unlawful arrest or detention shall have an enforceable right to compensation". Certainly, such legal procedures, systems and machinery were not at work during the mystical age in India.

Yudhistira in *Mahabharata* says: "who accompanies man in death?—*Dharma*" and the compensation to any evil deeds may be a miserable death.

Article 10, ICCPR reads: "All persons deprived of their liberty shall be treated with humanity and with respect for the inherent dignity of the human person". What is the inherent dignity of a human person?

"Man is the perfection of the creation" (*Chandogya Upanishad*, 2-6-1) and, therefore, he has the dignity which such a creation should have and man is created in the image of God. Any detinue needs to be treated with humanity, for, he does not lose his manness when he is under detention. Hence Pope thinks: "an honest man is the noblest work of God". Just enjoy what Cary tells:

"Knowing the right and true,
Let the world say to you
Worse than it can:
Answer despite the blame
Answer despite the shame,

I'll not belie my name—
I'll be a man"

and this is and should be the worth of a man. A man means a lot and contains a lot and precisely, therefore, he becomes the most perfect creation and that is the precise reason why he enjoys dignity. A crime-doer, an arrestee, a detinue, an accused, a convict—all have the dignity of a man and worth of a human person. Police cannot ignore it and if they ignore it, then they become human rights unfriendly resulting in adverse criticisms. Man is the only creation and he only may wish:

"O Pavamana, place me in the deathless, undecaying world wherein the light of heaven is set and everlasting lustre shines....in the third heaven where lucid words are full of light.....Make me immortal in that realm of eager, wish and strong desire.....make me immortal in that realm where happiness transports, where joys and facilities combine and longing wishes are fulfilled" (*Ṛg Veda* 10, 14 and 15 and also 9, 113). This is the worth of a man and there lies his dignity. Nobody can diminish the importance of man. Mystics in India realized this truth. Man is immortal in many ways and the police must acknowledge this fact. "It is by their own actions, good or bad, that men are happy or miserable" (Sukracharya in *Mahabharata*) and the police may realize that they can make people happy or unhappy by their own actions. United Nations want to make people and nations happy and that is why they bring out human rights declarations.

Article 12 of the Universal Declaration of Human Rights is reproduced under Article 17 of the ICCPR and to reiterate:

> "No one shall be subjected to arbitrary or unlawful interference with his privacy, family, home or correspondence, nor to unlawful attacks on his honour and reputation.
> "Everyone has the right to the protection of the law against such interference or attacks".

This article has been discussed at length elsewhere in this book. Nevertheless, it is necessary that the police must know the sanctity of a family. Pope Leo XIII says: "The family may be regarded as the cradle of civil society, and it is in great measure within the circle of family life that the destiny of States is fostered". If this is accepted, then there is no scope for interference in the family of a suspect/detinue/arrestee in criminal cases. How can the police interfere with the family and the private life of an individual unless it is essential for administering fair and just justice? Of course, there are a lot of criticisms against the police on this count and mainly it is because they are not fully aware of the sacredness of family in the protection of human rights. See what G.K. Chesterton says: "We can say that the family is the unit of the State; that it is the cell that makes up the formation. Round the family do indeed gather the sanctities that separate men from ants and bees. Decency is the curtain of the tent; liberty is the wall of that city; property is but the family harm; honour is but the family flag". The police must accept this fact when they investigate crimes, search families for the suspects, raid a family or interfere with the family members. The sanctity of marriage and family life was accepted and honoured in Indian mysticism.

> "O Agni, make perfect the
> wedded life of the wife and
> the husband by mutual concord
> and restraint, and do thou
> overpower the strength and
> energies of those who would
> be hostile to us"
>
> (*Ṛg Veda,* 5, 28, 3).

How can the police dishonour this sacred concept? The relationship between the wife and husband is so sacred that they do not want anyone to interfere in their family life.

"When my husband has not taken his food, I do not take food. When he has not bathed, I do not bath. When he does not rest himsėlf, I do not take rest, but remain engaged in my work" (Draupadi in *Van Parva*). There are allegations that some policemen torture the husbands in front of their wives and certainly, if it takes place, it is a heinous crime. There are further allegations that some policemen manhandle the father in front of the children. If the allegations are true, it is inhuman and against human dignity. Calling of epithets and uttering of indecent language to a person in front of his wife and children is against human decency and decorum.

The Indian mystical attitude to human rights (the term, however, was not used by the *ṛsis*) is quite interesting. The entire outlook to man and his rights was derived from intuition, experience and inward realization of Indian sages. Their vision is a kind of life or experience. It is an insight into the reality (*darsana*) or experience of reality (*anubhava*). The intuition, experience and insight carry their own credentials. What is said in Indian mysticism about human rights can be stated to be the vision of the soul and that is the precise reason why the mystical revelations are found to be having eternal values. The United Nations or for that purpose, any international bodies at any time cannot deviate from the eternal truths revealed in Indian mysticism and sacred scriptures. What is seen in the *Vedas*, the chief sacred scriptures of the Hindus, is and should be authoritative mystical experiences of *ṛsis*. The *Vedas* speak truths which the mystics experienced and the principles which underlie the human rights concepts. The human rights laws are proclaimed by the United Nations on the basis of an international consensus on the laws thus enacted. Certainly, the mystical revelations did influence the international thinking in humanizing the people. The saints of God saw realities much ahead of the world community. The mystics brought out revealed truths for those who were incapable of having the divine insight. Those who could not have vision wanted some formulae or rules of life which they desired sincerely. *Rsis* could give them and guide the world. The inspired truths did help many in the world to live a life respecting human dignity. The United Nations, through their efforts, have been trying to enforce the basic truths which people accepted even before the formation of the United Nations. The eternal truths do not and cannot come from vacuum. The testimony of the mystical sages was a sound assurance for the people of the world to enact all declarations for ensuring human rights. Precious as are the teachings of the revealed truths in the souls of *ṛsis*, the United Nations just recognized them and made them laws for guiding all people in all nations. God still reveals truth and United Nations may be one of the several ways the God reveals His wisdom. The people in the world—every creed, colour, culture, community, race—are the offsprings of God and if that is true, one must admit that human rights are universally applicable to every human being. The *Upanishad* says that "God, the maker of all, the great spirit ever seated in the hearts of creatures, is fashioned by the heart, the understanding and the will. They who know that become immortal" (*Svetasvatara Upanishad,* IV, 17).

5

Convention against Torture, Police and Indian Mysticism

Torture in the Random House College Dictionary means "the act of inflicting excruciating pain, esp. as a means of punishment or coercion". *An eye for an eye, a tooth for a tooth*—this approach based on the retributive justice was in vogue from time immemorial. Punishment was awarded to crime-doers with vindictive mind. Hence it was called *'lex talionis'* or law of retaliation. Humanitarian approaches and human rights laws insisted that crime-doers might be approached with humaneness. Afterall crime is a human act and as the Buddha affirms: "Never in the world will hatred cease by hatred...hatred is ceased by love" Likewise, never in the world will "crime be corrected by crime". "Let a man overcome anger by kindness, evil by good"—says the Buddha.

At the outset, one is confronted by the difficulty of defining what torture is in human rights laws. Hence, United Nations themselves have offered a description in their Convention Against Torture and Other Cruel, Inhuman or Degrading Treatment or Punishment (General Assembly Resolution 39/46). According to the Convention, *torture* means "any act by which severe pain or suffering, whether physical or mental, is intentionally inflicted on a person for such purposes as obtaining from him or a third person information or a confession, punishing him for an act he or a third person has committed or is suspected of having committed or intimidating or coercing him or a third person or for any reason based on discrimination of any kind, when such pain or suffering is inflicted by or at the instigation of or with the consent or acquiescence of a public official or other person acting in an official capacity. It does not include pain or suffering arising only from, inherent in or incidental to lawful sanctions". The definition seems to be very academic in its content.

The Indian mystical attitude to the causing of pain to anybody for any purpose is quite revealing. The mystical seers in India spoke out of their conviction that torture of any kind on human beings was bad. I may reiterate what is seen in *Manu Smriti*—

> "Forbearance, forgiveness,
> self control, non-stealing,
> purity, control of senses,
> virtuous intellect, knowledge,
> truthfulness, absence of
> anger are the ten laws
> of righteousness" (*Manu Smriti,* 6, 92)

It means that long before the world community passed a resolution against torture, there were spiritual utterances in India and they emphatically condemned torture of any kind on people. The echoes of God's voice came out from the mystical souls so much so that the world community could not but accept those precious truths in due course. In the 93rd plenary meeting held on 10 December, 1984, the United Nations emphatically said: "considering the obligation of States under the Charter, in particular Article 55, to promote universal respect for, and observance of human rights and fundamental freedoms.

Having regard to Article 5 of the Universal Declaration of Human Rights and Article 7 of the International Covenant on Civil and Political Rights, both of which provide that no one shall be subjected to torture or to cruel, inhuman or degrading treatment or punishment" and the nations in the world agreed to proclaim the Convention Against Torture and Other Cruel, Inhuman or Degrading Treatment or Punishment. Indian mystics had the intuition of man becoming inhuman to man and they uttered eternal truths for the guidance of humanity. They thought that all people in the world—down the centuries—needed the inspired wisdom to reach harmony and world peace by respecting human dignity of other fellow brethren.

"One should always behave towards all other creatures, as he should towards himself" (*Mahabharata, Shanti Parva,* 167, 9) and if that was the divine revelation, how could the people employ torture on others?—how could the people behave in a cruel, inhuman or degrading manner to fellow beings for obtaining information or a confession? Allegations are plenty that law enforcement officers, particularly the police, resort to torture, coercion, inhuman methods to obtain a confession or information from suspects, arrestees, detinues and so on. Police officers are public servants and being public officials or persons acting in an official capacity are not justified to have recourse to inhuman and degrading treatment. People give pay to them not for becoming people unfriendly in their approaches, but to become human rights friendly in all their transactions with people who often become helpless or defenceless before them.

> "Let every hand give
> comfort to all living
> beings and let it be
> the giver of health
> to the whole mankind" (*Ṛg Veda* 10, 137-7).

This was the Indian thought and in such a culture, torture and degrading treatments have no scope at all. People who behave in an inhuman way are spiritually dead, physically animal—like, functionally inhuman and officially intolerable.

"Abstention from injury is the highest religion. It is, again, the highest penance. It is also the highest truth from which all duty proceeds" (*Mahabharata, Anushasana Parva,* 115, 25).

The U.N. Convention Against Torture is mainly intended to protect the interests of crime-doers while they are dealt with by police and other sub-systems in justice administration. Before proceeding further, to quote:

"Whoever is kind to the creation, God is kind to him.

Therefore, be kind to man on the earth whether he be good or bad and being kind to the bad is to withhold them from badness" (*Hadis*). What is there to feel so big in being or becoming very good to a good man? If one does not become good to a good man, then he is a beast. Hence, it goes without saying that one must be good to the sinner, to the evil-minded, to the crime-doer, to the suspects, to the detinues, to the arrestees who are more often than not defenceless and helpless before the mammoth law enforcement agencies. Hence the United Nations insist "Each State Party shall take effective legislative, administrative, judicial or other measures to prevent acts of torture in any territory under its jurisdiction". Many nations including India have taken many steps—legislative, administrative and judicial to prevent acts of torture. Nevertheless, one doubts very much whether or not such steps taken are really effective to stop the malady! A number of custodial violence is reported. Still people die in police/judicial custody. The press reports the incidents and the number of cases initiated against public officials for alleged acts of violence/torture is on the increase and what is to be done? The complaints against police to authorities including the Human Rights Commissions too are on the increase. Where is the defect? The answer to the question may be seen in Indian mystical thoughts. The mystical inspirations have travelled many centuries and made great conquests. The thoughts continue to traverse even today as they have been for four or five millenniums. The duty of the public officials is not torturing the public, but to administer fair justice in a just manner.

"Good men are those who are forbearing and compassionate, who are friends to all beings and for whom there has never been any foe, who are mild and for whom their character is the ornament" (*Bhagavata, Kapila Avatara*). A law enforcement officer must be compassionate and should never be brutal. He must be the friend of both law abiding and law violating citizens. The character is very important and a person is said to possess good character if he has an upright conscience. A police officer who has an upright conscience can never become human rights unfriendly. For today, it is not the rule of law, but the rule of justice that is honoured. Many things which may be justified under a rule of law are not justified under a rule of justice. A police officer who is more concerned with the rule of law may ignore the rule of justice. There one may see miscarriage of justice and it may be done through torture, or through cruel, inhuman and degrading treatment.

> "A man is not just, if he carries a matter by violence" (*Dhammapada,* 19).

If at all the existing law is violated to administer justice, there is no harm in it. For "God protects him, who is just and truthful and destroys him who is not so" (*Ṛg Veda* 7, 104, 12). In many instances, the existing laws administer justice and in a few instances, the existing law administers injustice. More than that, the manner in which the existing law is executed decides the nature of justice administered. Police officers, it seems, are not concerned with the manner in which the law is administered as they are found to be over-concerned with the execution of the law in any way they want. The mystics do not favour such an attitude and approach and that is the precise reason why in *Ṛg Veda,* the God's seer says: "The heaven and earth sustain a justice loving man" (*Ṛg Veda* 3, 26, 9). The United Nations too subscribe the same view when they said:

> "No exceptional circumstances whatsoever, whether a state of war or a threat of war, internal political instability or any other public emergency, may be invoked as a justification of torture.
>
> "An order from a superior officer or a public authority may not be invoked as a justification of torture" [Article 2 (2 and 3) of the Convention against Torture].

Here justice alone is of paramount importance. "Those who do justice will be seen sitting on the right hand of God in radiant and glowing minarets on the day of resurrection. These are the people who acted justly in their domestic and other affairs"

(*Hadis*). Being guided by the mystical thoughts originated in India and by a culture developed here, India has enacted many laws for preventing torture in police work. As early as 1855, Torture Commission was appointed. There are provisions in the Indian Penal Code, 1860, Code of Criminal Procedure Code, 1861 (Also 1973) and in Indian Evidence Act, 1872 and they want to prevent torture by police. It means that the world consensus against torture was in existence much before—over a century—the United Nations proclaimed their Convention Against Torture during 1984.

Torture as an Offence under Law and Police

Article 4 in the Convention Against Torture is about torture as an offence under law and it reads:

> "Each State party shall ensure that all acts of torture are offences under its criminal law. The same shall apply to an attempt to commit torture and to an act by any person which constitutes complicity or participation in torture.
> "Each State party shall make these offences punishable by appropriate penalties which take into account their grave nature".

India has already made all acts of torture by police as offences under her criminal laws. Why do the police employ torture? The reasons may be many. One reason may be that the policeman does not see "God" in others. Policeman too is a "god", but he does not recognize that fact. *Dharma* in Indian mysticism is *right action* and whenever a policeman employs torture, he is not doing his "*dharma*". Justice must be administered in ways of righteousness (*dharma*) and not through torture or by unfair practices. Torture is an evil in police work, an error in administration of justice and an ugliness in showing respect to human rights and to the dignity of man. The Indian mystics do not consider any man as an absolute evil so as to deserve torture. If anyone uses torture in the pretext of administering justice, to that extent the justice administration is a failure. If administration of justice is a divine duty, employment of torture is an act of the devil. Fair and just justice is divine and if it can be ensured in a perfect way—total justice—equal justice—then that perfection is supremely divine. The mystical thought is "whatsoever is glorious, good, beautiful and mighty, understand that it goes forth from out of a fragment of any splendour" (*Bhagavad Gita,* X, 41). The wages of using torture, third degree methods, coercion etc.... to a suspect in police custody are found to be ill-name for the whole police.

Indian laws punish not only torture by police, but also any attempt to torture. In some instances, the police may be able to do many things in a clandestine way. It being the case, the people today demand more transparency of police actions. There is a view that policeman who respects the brotherhood of man will never employ torture on suspects. Calvin Coolidge says: "our doctrine of equality and liberty and humanity comes from our belief in the brotherhood of man, through the fatherhood of God". Human rights activists advocate this brotherhood of man and the mystical revelations of India accepted it long-long ago.

> "O God, Thou are our
> father, our brother, our
> friend" (*Sama Veda*)

If this was the vedic revelation, then universal brotherhood was honoured by the mystics in India.

> "Bounteous one, Thou art our
> Father; and our mother,
> O Lord, Thou hast been" (*Ṛg Veda*, 8, 98, 11).

If fatherhood is accepted, the brotherhood too is accepted.

> As a mother her son,
> do thou protect us,
> grant to us prosperity
> and wisdom" (*Prasna Upanishad,* XIII).

United Nations' Convention Against Torture and Other Cruel, Inhuman or Degrading Treatment or Punishment is all about what each State Party must do to put down the torture and other Cruel, Inhuman or Degrading Treatment or Punishment. Indian mystics, on the other hand, speak about what each individual must do so that he can respect human dignity and rights. This indeed is a great difference between the two approaches. Unless the man changes, the desire of United Nations can never be changed. The mystics want to effect changes in man and for it they want to get divine interference. They analyse the root cause of human rights violations whereas the United Nations do not do so (?)

* "That man alone acquires strength of body and soul and attains happiness whose heart is free from suspicion and is filled with faith" (*Ṛg Veda*, 2, 26, 3).
* "The man with full of faith obtaineth wisdom, and he also hath mastery over his senses and having obtained wisdom he goeth swiftly to the Supreme Peace" (*Gita*, IV, 39).
* "If a man's faith is unsteady, if he does not know the true law, if his peace of mind is troubled, his knowledge will never be perfect" (*Dhammapada*).

Such an approach centering man to effect changes in him and thereby to create a new world order is not seen in United Nations' Declarations. United Nations feel, somehow or other, that a change is possible by enactment of laws and prescribing punishments for human rights violations. As the mystical visions are inspired ones, certainly they are superior to the United Nations' visions on human rights. Indian mysticism and its revealed teachings have converted millions and millions of people and brought them to the right direction. One doubts very much whether or not the United Nations can influence people and their thinking as much as the divinely inspired truths can do. The mystics invoke God's grace to achieve their objectives. Gandhiji once said: "Blast my faith in God and I am dead".

"Oh Lord, may I behold all the beings with the eye of a friend and may all the beings view me with kindly looks. May we all look at each other with the eye of a friend" (*Yajur Veda* 36, 18). When the mystics say so, the United Nations may proclaim:

"Each State Party shall ensure that education and information regarding the prohibition against torture are fully included in the training of law enforcement personnel, civil, military, medical personnel, public officials and other persons who may be involved in the custody, interrogation or treatment of any individual subjected to any form of arrest, detention or imprisonment" (Article 10, Convention Against Torture and Other Cruel, Inhuman and Degrading Treatment or Punishment). Of course, education and information can cause behavioural modification. Nevertheless, one doubts whether or not they will be as powerful as the mystical revelations which make a total change in the attitude, outlook and approach of the people. Dr. Radhakrishnan writes: "Hindu religion can be described in one word, that is, do the right" and the human rights declarations too say the same thing—but in a different way with a different approach. Farquar adds: "As long as the world lasts, men will look back with wonder upon the ascetics of India".

Hinduism is not only a religion. It is a way of life. It is a culture. It is a civilization. It contains *Dharma*. It means social practices. Hence, Indian mysticism too means all of them. It means equality, human dignity, worth of human person and what not? Hinduism and Indian mysticism—they have only one aim, namely, elevation of man to divine union. At the same time, the Declarations of the United Nations are just Declarations made by the Nations of the world. Nations of the world means many governments in power. People individually are not involved in the acceptance or implementation of the principles. As such, the mystical truths have decisive influence on the beliefs and behaviour of the people which the U.N. Declarations may not enjoy. Mahatma Gandhi once said: "If I were asked to define the Hindu creed I should simply say: search after truth through non-violent means. A man may or may not believe in God and still call himself a Hindu. Hinduism is a relentless pursuit after truth.... Hinduism is the religion of truth. Truth is God. Denial of God we have known. Denial of truth we have not known". United Nations' Declarations on human rights, certainly, are human attempts to establish the inviolable birth rights of people on an international basis. They, however, do not have the spiritual power which, of course, the mystical revelations do have. This is the difference.

Police as an agency to enforce justice and truth, have to implement human rights laws. Every policeman, when he enforces human rights laws—protects human rights—he enforces and protects the truths revealed by the Hindu seers and mystics. In *Taittriya Upanishad*, 1, 1, we read: "after having taught the *Vedas*, the teacher instructs the pupil thus: speak what is true. Do your duty". And what is this truth? It means enforcement of human rights as well.

"Every duty is holy and devotion to duty is the highest form of worship"—says Swami Vivekananda. The same approach can be taken by policemen too towards enforcement of human rights. Everything a policeman does towards the actualisation of human rights is holy and devotion to behave in a human rights friendly way is the highest form of loyalty in police work. Torture, cruel, inhuman and degrading treatments and punishments in police work are condemned and are looked down upon by the international community. Anything the policemen do for respecting the human dignity is a good action and is his duty. Whenever he behaves in a human rights unfriendly manner, his actions take him downward and, therefore, are bad in content and spirit. Precisely, therefore, they are not his duties.

How to inculcate the Indian mystical truths to policemen? These eternal truths, if inculcated to the policemen in the right perspectives, surely will make them to become more human rights friendly. Hinduism, Christianity, Buddhism, Islam — all these world religions have mystical revelations and all of them talk the same truth in different ways. All of them speak of human rights and worth of human persons. If the divine truths revealed by these religions are honestly taught to law enforcement agencies and people alike, doubtlessly they will become people friendly and thus a lot of conflicts and fights on the basis of caste, colour, creed and community can be reduced.

6

Children, Police, Human Rights and Mysticism

"Children are God's apostles, sent forth, day by day, to preach of love and hope and peace" (J.R. Lowell). Life's aspirations come in the guise of children" (Tagore). The first duty to children is to make them happy. If you have not made them so, you have wronged them. No other good they may get can make up for that" (Buxton). "When the child begins to pick up the alphabet, he should be initiated into the science of the soul" (Swami Dayanand) and thus speak many great men everywhere in the world. Naturally and necessarily, the children are important for policemen and every policeman must be a model for children.

Convention on the Rights of the Child proclaimed by the United Nations in their 61st plenary meeting held on 20th November, 1989 has reaffirmed: "Children's rights require special protection and call for continuous improvement of the situation of children all over the world, as well as for their development and education in conditions of peace and security". In India, Rabindra Nath Tagore said long back: "The object of education is the freedom of the mind, which can only be achieved through the path of freedom....though freedom has its risks and responsibility as life itself has." United Nations emphatically assert in the Convention on the Rights of the Child that "Childhood is entitled to special care and assistance" and the police have to bear them in mind when they interact with children. "I do not love him because he is good. I love him because he is my child"—Tagore said and this must and this alone must guide the police when they deal with children, no matter they are neglected, delinquent, abused, victimized, uncontrollable and incorrigible. Every child is a child to a policeman and the policeman must love him. Working with children is not a police job; it is a calling—a vocation and a divine mission. The police must think that "every child comes with the message that God is not yet discouraged of man" (Tagore) and if that is the truth, every child deserves to be treated as a person and with human dignity.

"I am the soul of all beings, am always present in all beings" (*Srimad Bhagvata*) and the truth is true in the case of all children—no matter they are crime-doers or law abiding. Every child is the child of God, the creator. "He is Vishwakarman, Maker, Disposer and most loftly preserver of the world" (*Ṛg Veda* X, 82). Importance of child was recognized in India from the Vedic period and children were given special status in Indian culture and civilization from time immemorial. Even delinquent children were legally respected and the Apprentices Act, 1850 had special provisions for children who committed offences. Special provisions in the Indian Penal Code, Code of Criminal Procedure, Reformatory Schools Act, Children Act etc. show that Indians did give special consideration, care, status etc. to children who were delinquent or neglected. Certainly, the Indian attitude was influenced by the mystical revelations and culture.

United Nations enacted Standard Minimum Rules for the Administration of Juvenile Justice (The Beijing Rules) (96th plenary meeting, 29th November, 1985), United Nations' Standard Minimum Rules for the Administration of Juvenile Justice (The Beijing Rules) (Economic and Social Council Resolution 1989/66, 15th plenary meeting, 24th May, 1989), United Nations' Guidelines for the Prevention of Juvenile Delinquency (The Riyadh Guidelines, General Assembly Resolution 45/112, 68th plenary meeting, 14th December, 1990) and United Nations' Rules for the Protection of Juveniles Deprived of their Liberty (General Assembly Resolution 45/113, 68th plenary meeting, 14th December, 1990). Moreover, the Convention on the Right of the Child (General Assembly Resolution, 44/25) was passed by the United Nations. All were done with an intention to protect the human rights of children in line with what had been revealed in mystical thoughts. It cannot be otherwise, for,

> "Thou art light O, God.
> Give me light" (*Yajur Veda* 19, 9)

Everything good comes from God.

"O omnipotent God! Thou art the sole Master of all mankind and the sole and supreme Ruler of the whole universe. Being such and, being praised by us, let thou flow upon us streams of such perfectly bliss—imparting wealth as will enable us to live in peace and happiness". (*Ṛg Veda* 6, 36, 4). United Nations and the world community want peace and harmony in the world and for that the human rights must be respected. Mysticism, whether it is Indian or Eastern, contains eternal truths and the United Nations bring them out to international attention. Like Hinduism and Buddhism, Taoism is full of intuitive wisdom and it contains a lot of principles accepted by United Nations for promoting human rights. Taoism believed in good and bad and they are interrelated in the same way as YIN and YANG. The Taoist mysticism tries to maintain a dynamic balance between good and bad.

"Shall we not follow and honour the right and have nothing to do with the wrong?" (Chaung Tzu). The United Nations and the international community are pursuing the paths of mystical revelations in all their activities to establish human rights. As this book deals only with Indian mystical wisdom, nothing seen in other eastern mystical thoughts is discussed here. Again, as this book deals with human rights, police and Indian mysticism, the discussion is limited only to those areas.

In administering juvenile justice, United Nations want protection and promotion of the rights of the young and precisely, therefore, they state:

"Recognizing that the young, owing to their early stage of human development, require particular care and assistance with regard to physical, mental, social development and require legal protection in conditions of peace, freedom, dignity and security".

Indian mystical sages too wanted peace in the world and in *Yajur Veda* (36, 17), it is seen:

"Peace of sky, peace of mid-region, peace of earth, peace of waters, peace of plants....Peace of *Brahman*, peace of the universe, peace of peace, may that peace come to me". What more does one need? The saints knew that people have to preserve the forces of nature within themselves to keep peace.

"Those who love and keep peace, preserve the forces of nature (physical, mental and spiritual) within themselves" (*Atharva Veda*, 19, 27, 10). This is what the United Nations want the world community to do for administering justice including juvenile justice.

What must the police do to ensure juvenile justice? According to United Nations—

"The Juvenile Justice system shall emphasize the well-being of the juvenile and shall ensure that any reaction to juvenile offenders shall always be in proportion to the circumstances of both the offenders and the offence". The well-being of people has always been given high importance in India. Mahatma Gandhi said about education: "Education is an all-round drawing out of the best in the child and man—body, mind and spirit". The United Nations have just applied this principle in juvenile justice administration. The police, as a sub-system in the juvenile justice administration, has a duty of a teacher as well and every police officer/man must play a constructive role for the well-being of a juvenile.

Protection of Privacy

The United Nations say: "The juvenile's right to privacy shall be respected at all stages in order to avoid harm being caused to her or him by undue publicity or by the process of labelling.

In principle, no information that may lead to the identification of a juvenile offender shall be published". After all a juvenile is a juvenile and he/she has the immaturity of understanding. Why should his/her name be published? Every child has a future and it must not be destroyed by undue publicity. Police must not make the names of the juvenile offender public, for, the objectives of juvenile justice administration is correction and rehabilitation of children.

"Let thy speech be pure, forceful and sweet"
(*Atharva Veda* 16, 2, 9).

Of course, in *Srimad Bhagavata*: Ajamala, it is seen: "All those who commit sin deserve punishment in accordance with what they have done". But, even in punishing a man, one must be decent and human rights friendly. The most important characteristic of the Indian mystical view is the awareness of all these truths although the sages did not talk in the tongue of the world community today. Juvenile justice administration, police etc. may not be known to them as they are known now. Nevertheless, they had the inspired vision of all these latest concepts. They knew the criminal's mind and the mind of the policeman. They said: "When we men, O Varuna, commit an offence before the heavenly host, when we break the law through thoughtlessness, have mercy on us, Almighty, have mercy on us" (*Ṛg Veda* 1, 25).

The world community knows that many police functionaries are unaware of the juvenile psychology, methods of dealing with children who find difficulty with law etc. Hence, the United Nations insist training and instruction to juvenile justice personnel.

"In order to best fulfil their functions, police officers who frequently or exclusively deal with juveniles or who are primarily engaged in the prevention of juvenile crime shall be specially instructed and trained. In large cities, special police units should be established for that purpose". The idea of imparting knowledge through instructions is as old as Indian mysticism.

"One ignorant of the land asks of one who knows it; he travels forward instructed by knowing guide. This indeed is the blessing of instruction; one finds the path that leads straight onwards" (*Rg Veda* 10, 32, 7). In spite of mystical wisdom and United Nations' desire, most frustratingly enough, no such special trainings or specialized instructions are imparted to Indian Police in a purposive manner—says the critic.

The parallels between juvenile delinquency, police job, juvenile justice and mystical experiences may not be seen unless one tries to read the revealed truths in the light of the latest concepts and world views of crimes committed by children and justice administered by the authorities. In Part VI—Legislation and Juvenile Justice Administration—in the United Nations' Guidelines for the Prevention of Juvenile Delinquency (The Riyadh Guidelines), it is laid down:

"Governments should enact and enforce specific laws and procedure to promote and protect the rights and well-being of all young persons".

Again it is stated:

"Legislation preventing the victimization, abuse, exploitation and the use for criminal activities of children and young persons should be enacted and enforced". Accordingly a number of legislations has come into being and the police are given a lot of power to deal with the situations.

Indian mystical saints too say the same thing, but they do not entrust the responsibility on States and Governments. They entrust the same to a strong power.

> "And, O Strong One, whenever mortal knowingly
> injures another mortal by falsehood from
> such a one, O praised Agni, protect him who
> praises Thee" (*Ṛg Veda* 1, 147, 5)

Victimization, abuse, exploitation and the use for criminal activities, they believed, could be prevented thus. "Evil befalls him who doth evil" (*Atharva Veda,* 10, 1, 5) and the legislations which the Governments make today are intended to punish those who violate human rights. The mystics could foresee the evil that might fall on the evil-doers. If the police do evil, they too will suffer the ill-effects of their evil behaviour. Hence—

> "Give up all evil even here" (*Atharva Veda,* 12, 2, 27)

> "A man of evil thoughts endangers hatred
>
> which brings misery" (*Uttradhain Sutra,* 32, 18)

> "A man is made miserable by his own thoughts"
> (*Uttradhain Sutra*, 9, 51).

Hence, as the United Nations say: "No child or young person should be subjected to harsh or degrading correction or punishment measures at home, in schools or in any other institutions". This is applicable to the police and to the police stations where children are brought to administer justice.

Juveniles deprived of their Liberty

United Nations' Rules for the Protection of Juveniles Deprived of their Liberty reads:

"Alarmed at the conditions and circumstances under which juveniles are being deprived of their liberty world wide.

Aware that juveniles deprived of their liberty are highly vulnerable to abuse, victimization in goals and facilities with adults, the United Nations want that children must receive "special attention and protection and that their rights and well-being should be guaranteed".

The United Nations say: "Recourse to instruments of restraint and to force for any purpose should be prohibited" and the police, therefore, cannot handcuff the juveniles. This is intended as a protection against humiliation and degradation for, both are human rights violations. Police have to maintain decorum when they deal with hard-core criminals and, therefore, it goes without saying that they must be doubly conscious of keeping the decorum when they deal with children. Tirukkural says: "Observe decorum, if good name you seek". Tagore reminds that "civility is a beauty of behaviour" and handcuffing the juveniles is not considered as civility in police service. Any police officer who becomes harsh to children is an evil-doer and he is under the influence of his evil propensities. He injures thereby the God, the Almighty. I quote again from *Ṛg Veda:* "He, who under the influence of his evil propensities injures me or intends to injure me, is injured himself by his own wickedness and evil nature, then why should I retaliate? (*Ṛg Veda* 8, 18, 13).

Every police officer/man must be aware of the rights of the child so that he can mould his behaviour accordingly.

Rights of the Child

United Nations' Convention on the Rights of the Child under Article 3 reads:

> "In all actions concerning children whether undertaken by public or private social welfare institutions, courts of law, administrative authorities or legislative bodies the best interest of the child shall be a primary consideration".

Police comes here under the administrative authorities and precisely, therefore, the police must know what really are the best interests of children. Indian sages have said:

"Truth, self control, asceticism, generosity, non-violence, constancy in virtue"—acquisition of them are and must be the best interest of children—says *Mahabharata* (3, 181, 42).

> "Virtue should be the aim and end
> Of every life, all else in vain,
> Duty should be its dearest friend
> If higher life it would attain" (Toru Dutt)

And any attempt initiated and implemented by police to inculcate virtues, duty consciousness and human qualities will be considered as good actions done for the best interest of children.

Article 17 of the Convention of the Rights of the Child is all about torture, cruel or degrading treatment or punishment and it reads:

"State Parties shall ensure that:

(a) No child shall be subjected to torture or other cruel, inhuman or degrading treatment or punishment. Neither capital punishments nor life imprisonment without possibility of release shall be imposed for offences committed by persons below eighteen years of age.

(b) No child shall be deprived of his or her liberty unlawfully or arbitrarily. The arrest, detention or imprisonment of a child shall be in conformity with the law and shall be used only as a measure of last resort and for the shortest appropriate period of time.

(c) Every child deprived of liberty shall be treated with humanity and respect for the inherent dignity of human person and in a manner which takes into account the needs of person and of his or her age. In particular, every child deprived of liberty shall be separated from adults unless it is considered in the child's best interest not to do so and shall have the right to maintain contacts with his or her family through correspondence and visits, save in exceptional circumstances".

A reading into the article of the Convention shows that a child deserves human treatment with mercy and consideration.

"He is merciful to him, who has committed sin" (*Ṛg Veda* 7, 87, 7) and sin is a violation of the God's law. Crime is a violation of State's law and the State cannot take an approach which the Supreme Law giver does not take. He is merciful and the United Nations repeat the same thing when they say that "no child shall be subjected to torture, or other cruel, inhuman or degrading treatment or punishment". The police can never and must, by no means, resort to any inhuman strategies when children are dealt with. The Supreme Law Giver is the supreme executor of law and no policeman/officer is bigger than the Supreme Law Giver and the executor. For, He is the Friend, Father, Fatherliest of fathers" (*Ṛg Veda* 4, 17, 17).

Why should a child—if at all he is a law-breaker—must be tortured?—cruelly and inhumanely treated?—or given degrading and cruel punishments? There is no justification for it and the world community does not accept it. As the executor of law, the society must show mercy to children and do only those things which are to the interest of children—and nothing more.

"Invaluable are His mercies and His commands"

—Guru Nanak.

"His infinite mercy is open to everyone" —Vivekananda

The world community is not in favour of enforcing death penalty and, therefore, it goes without saying that the children should not be sentenced to capital punishment. The United Nations subscribe to the view of abolishing death penalty—and more so in the case of children. Every sinner—every crime-doer—must be provided with sufficient time for repentance and the mystical revelation too is for providing time for repentance.

"May the gods who are all knowing, the lords of everything, animate and inanimate, help us to go beyond our sins committed and uncommitted (*i.e.,* past and future) for our ultimate good" (*Ṛg Veda* 63, 8) and by inflicting capital punishment, the opportunity to repent is denied. This is a human rights violation and the policemen must not be instrumental to it.

No arbitrary or unlawful arrest of children—this is what the U.N. Convention says. They shall be resorted even in the rarest of rare occasions or even when no other method is available. Imprisonment is intended for correcting the delinquent and if release is not allowed, then correction becomes meaningless. A child has many years to live and if allowed, he may change his law violating tendencies and behaviour.

"A man becomes good by good deeds, and bad by bad deeds" (*Brihadaranyaka Upanishad* III, 2, 13) and if that is a mystical thought, then there is scope of child development provided appropriate environment is provided. A delinquent child should not be denied of opportunities to become good. He must not be exposed to situations which humiliate him or which are human rights unfriendly. Police must not be instrumental to such degrading and inhuman acts. The United Nations emphatically say (Article 16) that "no child shall be subjected to arbitrary or unlawful interference with his or her privacy, family, home or correspondence, nor to unlawful attacks on his or her honour and reputation".

The current words like delinquency, arbitrary arrests, human dignity etc. may not be seen in the mystical revelations. At the same time, the mystical seers could get the revelation about many things that would come after several thousands of years. The revealed truths were the visions of the soul and they could never be incorrect. The sages experienced realities and brought them out for many generations. The United Nations, when they enacted human rights declarations, were proclaiming nothing but everything which the mystical seers stated long—very long back. This is the reason why Farquar says and to quote him once again: "As long as the world lasts men will look back with wonder upon the ascetics of India". Dr. S. Radhakrishnan writes: "Hindu religion can be described in one word, that is—do the right". Swami Vivekananda says: "All will agree on the point that we believe the *Vedas* to be the eternal teachings" and these are what great men speak about Hinduism, mysticism and Indian revelations etc. Then it goes without saying that the human rights concepts which people talk in loud voice now are the property of Indian mystical thoughts. Certainly, they may be seen in other mystical writings, but there exist no research studies on the subject. Buddhism, Taoism etc., may have rich teachings on human rights, but they become outside the search of this book.

> "He alone knows adequately what rectitude is;
> who knows the 'ought' and the 'ought not'".
>
> (*Gita* 46, 15, 17)

> "O Lord, grant me that intellect by getting
> which I may not forget Thee and grant me that
> wisdom by which I may always remember Thee"
>
> (Majh Mohalla, 5)

7

Women, Human Rights, Police and Mysticism

How do the Mystics in India see Women and their Rights?

There is a Sanskrit verse: "Wherever women are revered, there gods reside". Manu says: "Where women are honoured, gods are happy. Where women are not respected, all efforts come to naught". India has a tradition and culture of respecting women and again Manu says: "that family is foredoomed where women are in grief". Family means and includes husband and wife with or without children and India had the joint family system wherein people of different generations lived happily and in harmony.

"In the destruction of a family, immemorial family traditions perish; in the perishing of traditions, lawlessness overcomes the whole family....this confusion draggeth to hell the slayers of the family and the family" (*Bhagavad Gita*, 1, 40 and 42). Women play a noble role in Indian family set-up and she is respected everywhere as a "goddess" in Indian mysticism. Police have to acknowledge this fact and they must show supreme respect to women and their gender when they interact with women and girls in various capacities. Whenever police had misbehaved with women, they had to face public hostility and adverse criticisms. Misbehaving with women is not there in Indian culture and tradition although people show, in live situations, disrespect to women in many ways. The reasons are, probably, sociological and not at all religious and mystical in origin.

> "Lo verily, not for love of the husband is a husband dear, but for the love of the *Atman* a husband is dear.
> Lo verily, not for the love of the wife is a wife dear, but for the love of the *Atman* a wife is dear.
> Lo verily, not for love of the sons are sons dear, but for the love of the *Atman* sons are dear" (*Brihadaranyaka Upanishad,* 11, 4, 1, 3).

The mystical truth shows that *Atman* is present in the husband, wife and sons and all are equal. There is no discrimination on the basis of sex and status between husband and wife and in that sense one sees respect to human rights in a supreme way.

Article 2 of the Universal Declaration of Human Rights makes it clear that all human rights are for all without distinction of any kind on the basis of sex. This coincides with the Indian mystical teachings which accept the truth that every human being—man and woman—has an individuality worthy of reverence. However, a lot of stories are heard against police. They are accused of misbehaving with women showing no reverence as taught by the mystical seers in India. According to Dr. S. Radhakrishnan, "Siva is *ardhanarisvara,* and his image signifies the co-operative, interdependent, separately incomplete but jointly complete masculine and feminine functions of the Supreme Being". What a sublime idea! Dr. Radhakrishnan continues:

"Man is not a tyrant nor is woman a slave, but both are servants of a higher ideal to which their individual inclinations are to be subordinated. Sensual love is sublimated into self-forgetful devotion". This is the mystical view of Hinduism. Relationship of Rama and Sita or Savitri and Satyavan—they stand together—in equal dignity—and they are idealized in Hindu scriptures. The world community, through their Conventions and Declarations, speaks the same thing on an international platform.

Women come to police stations in different capacities and the police are expected to deal with them with gender dignity.

Though indecent behaviours towards women by police come in the media—sometimes in an exaggerated form—studies show that gender indecency shown to men by police may be more than what they show to women. No matter, the indecent behaviour is shown towards man or woman, every indecent behaviour is a human rights violation showing inhuman and degrading treatment. Neither United Nations nor the mystical teachings, nor human rights laws nor the world community, nor any civilization, nor the civilized laws, nor the courts, nor the people can tolerate such cruel acts. Whenever the wickedness of showing sexual indecency to woman comes into being, people have a tendency to exaggerate the wickedness to an alarming size. People respond to such acts of police in total disfavour and hatred. According to Indian thoughts, women are having an exalted status and it must be recognized by male dominated police service. She is the helpmate of man in all his work and the policeman must not forget that fact. As she is the helpmate of man, she is respectfully addressed as *sahadharmini* and this view has been well brought out in *Ṛg Veda* (V. 61.8) and it reads:

"The wife and the husband, being the equal halves of the substance, are equal in every respect; both should join and take equal part in all work—religious and secular". Calling epithets to women or uttering indecent words to women or speaking in filthy language etc... are infamies and must never be resorted to them when they are in police custody or when they are having interactions with police. They are infamies indeed! Prostitutes have human dignity and they insist human rights friendly approaches from police everywhere. The prostitute—currently known as a sex worker—if I may say so, is losing herself respect. She herself does not respect her sex as she entertains promiscuous sex relationship. Of course, her lack of self-respect and sex-values cannot be brought as a ground to justify gender indecency with women by police.

Article 16 of the Universal Declaration of Human Rights is as under:

"Men and women of full age, without any limitation due to

> race, nationality or religion have the right to marry and to found a family. They are entitled to equal rights as to marriage, during marriage and at its dissolution.
>
> "Marriage shall be entered into only with the free and full consent of the intending spouses.
>
> "The family is the natural and fundamental group unit of society and is entitled to protection by society and the State".

The Hindu mysticism is full of the ideas expressed by United Nations under Article 16, U.D.H.R. Right to marry and the right to found a family are accepted by the sacred scriptures in Hinduism.

"The whole duty, in brief, of husband and wife towards each other is that they cross not and wander not apart from each other in thought, word and deed until death" (Manu, *Dharma-Sastra*, IX, 96). Perhaps, the Indian thoughts are far superior in contents and meaning than what they are in U.D.H.R. In *Ṛg Veda* (8, 31, 5, 9), it is seen:

> "Gods, may the husband and wife, who with one mind purify the libations and offer them to us...may they constantly be associated....never be wanting in food. Blessed with youthful and adolescent offspring...they pass happily their whole life".
>
> "O Agni, make perfect the wedded life of the wife and the husband by mutual concord and restraint, and do thou overpower the strength and energies of those who would be hostile to us" (*Ṛg Veda* 5, 28, 3).

Reading through the mystical revelations, one may understand that the inspiration is for a married life until death. Divorce, dissolution etc. are not contemplated. The United Nations make the right for dissolution too a human right for man and woman.

"I seize thy hand for the great good fortune that thou mayest live with me, as thy husband till decay comes upon thee" (*Ṛg*

Veda, 10, 85, 34). This is Hindu vision and the United Nations being moved by the current social conditions and deteriorated family values have made the right to dissolution too a human right which can be enjoyed both by man and woman equally. Dr. Radhakrishnan writes:

> "We have no time to understand one another. To justify our conduct, we are setting up exaggerated claim on behalf of the individual will and are strongly protesting against discipline. We are confusing self-expression and self-development with a life of instincts and passions. We tend to look upon ourselves as healthy animals and not spiritual beings. We have had sin with us from the beginning of our history, but we have recently begun to worship it. It is not very modern for a man or woman who is sick of his or her partner to take to another but what is really modern is the new philosophy in justification of it. Disguised feeling is masquerading as advanced thought. The woman who gives up her husband for another is idealized as a heroine who has had the courage to give up the hypocritical moral codes and false sentiments while she who clings to her husband through good report and bad is a cowardly victim of conventions. Sex irregularities are becoming less shocking and more popular".

According to U.N. Declarations, men and women have equal rights for marriage and its dissolution. But, the mystical seers think about marriage as a sacred relation between man and woman until their death. It being the case, the question of divorce and the equal right for divorce do not arise. Just listen to what Savitri in *Vana Parva* says: "Be he, long-lived or short-lived, endowed with good qualities or utterly lacking in them, once my husband has been chosen by me, I will not choose another". The police may receive petitions of family quarrels and domestic violence and usually the police may try their best to amicably settle the issues. If they fail in their attempts, they may refer the matter to some counselling centres as they do not want to see that they separate themselves. They are moved more by the inspired mysticism than the human rights declarations. The police officers often quote from Indian scriptures and tell the couples to find out an amicable settlement.

> "Noble lady, even if my
> husband is devoid of good
> conduct, yet he must be
> served without any hesitation
> by me" (Sita in *Valmiki Ramayana*)

> "There is no other holy tasks,
> prescribed for a woman,
> than attendance on her
> husband. Savitri attended
> on her husband and was
> honoured in heaven" (Sita in *Valmiki Ramayana*)

The police officers do not, often, speak much or anything about Divorce Acts or Human Rights. For, they consider that marriage, family, children etc. should be seen beyond, besides and above human rights and Divorce Act. King Janaka said to Rama: "here is my daughter, Sita, who will tread with you the path of *dharma*. Take her hand in yours; blessed and devoted, she will ever walk with you like your own shadow".

Article 25, U.D.H.R. is about the right to a standard of living adequate for the health and well-being of oneself and of his family. It also speaks about the right to security in the event of widowhood. The article continues: "Motherhood and childhood are entitled to special care and assistance".

In Indian tradition and culture, a woman is looked after by her father—by her husband—and by her children. She is well protected. During the wedding ceremony, it is recited:

> "The sky is firm, the whole
> world is firm, the mountains
> are firm in her husband's
> family...I bind your
> heart and mind with a

knot of truth. May your
heart be mine; may
my heart be yours".

India is a country where *Sati* was practised and now there is Sati Prevention Act in force to protect the interest of widows. According to Indian custom, a widow must be looked after by her husband's family after the death of her husband. The United Nations make it a human right to offer a right to security in the event of widowhood. Instances are plenty to show that widows come to police stations with complaints of harassment, victimization, torturing and lack of security. In many occasions, police become helpless to provide immediate or adequate remedy for their problems. Motherhood and childhood are entitled to special care and assistance. The police face some problems when a woman having a child (breast-feeding) comes as a detinue in police custody. Naturally and necessarily, such a detinue deserves special care and assistance. There is a proverb and it is: "A mother's heart is always with her children" and it is true in the case of every woman, no matter she is a convict, a detinue or a suspect in a crime.

International Covenant on Economic, Social and Cultural Rights, Women and Police

ICESCR in Article 3 says: "The State Parties to the present Covenant undertake to ensure the equal right of men and women to the enjoyment of all economic, social and cultural rights set forth in the present Covenant". Men and women have equal rights and this was repeatedly accepted by Indian mysticism. Nevertheless, Indians give some special rights and privileges to women although some of them claim now that the women are a suppressed community or oppressed group in Indian society. India is a male dominated society—*'patriarchy'* system—and precisely, therefore, men become more powerful than women and they deny some of the rights which women ought to enjoy in India. Like patriarchy in some communities, there exists matriarchy in some other communities. In such communities, the women are more powerful than men and they deny some of the rights which men ought to enjoy. All said and done, the police in India treat women as weaker sections of the society. They are treated as a sexually handicapped group. Apart from the National Commission for Women established at Delhi, there are State Women's Commissions deeply engaged in the women's uplifment and empowerment. The functions of a State Women's Commission as given in a State Women's Commission Act are:

1. inquire into any unfair practice, take decision thereon;
2. cause investigations on issues concerning unfair practices;
3. identify lacunae, inadequacies or shortcomings in the laws in force which affect the Constitutional right to equality and fair treatment of women;
4. monitor of the working of laws in force concerning women with a view to identify the areas where the enforcement of laws is not adequately effective or has not been streamlined.

"Unfair practice" is defined in the Act and it means "any distinction, exclusion or restriction made on the basis of sex for the purpose of or which has the effect of impairing or nullifying the recognition, enjoyment or exercise by women of fundamental, Constitutional rights, or of human rights, or of fundamental freedom in the political, economic, social, cultural, civil or any other field or the infringement of any right or benefit conferred on women by or under the provisions of any law for the time being in force or the mental or physical torture or sexual excesses on women".

The Women's Commission Act and the provisions contained therein show that women do not enjoy equal right with men whatever may be the inspired or mystical teachings on the subject. The parallels, in United Nations' proclamations and in Indian mystical revelations on the subject may be the same, yet, the fact remains that the women suffer a lot in many ways—so much so that the legislatures in various States and the Parliament thought of passing Women's Commission Acts to safeguard and protect the interest and rights of women in India. The Acts speak about human rights violations against women and empower the Women's Commission to inspect prisons, police stations, lock-ups, sub-jails, rescue homes or other places of custody where women are kept as prisoners or otherwise, or shelters for women or other places run by the Government or any of its agencies including rescue or shelter to women, or hostels intended for women or girls run by any person and such other places wherein unfair practice to women is complained of and cause further inquiries to be made about the treatment that women and girls are subjected to at such places and to report to the Government for taking remedial actions". Of course, men and women are equal under the Indian Constitution and the laws made thereunder. There are any number of parallels in Indian mysticism and international laws to assert that men and women are equal in their rights. Nevertheless in practice, there exists a lot of discrimination between man and woman and one may see a number of unfair practices in existence in India. Police, jails, lock-ups, rescue homes, women's hostels etc. are not free from such unfair practices. What a tragedy indeed!

Indian culture always respected women. Chanakya says: "He who looks upon all women as his own mother...is a truly learned man". It means that the women were given a higher status—the status of a mother.

"Guard yourself against looking on a woman. If you see a woman, let it be as though you saw her not, and have no conversation with her" (The Buddha).

How could the culture which always respected gender dignity and women's status become one which allowed unfair practices? The mystics never wanted it. According to the Buddha:

> "If the woman be old
> regard her as your mother;
> If young, as your sister;
> if very young, as your child".

Rape, molestation, adultery, eve-teasing etc. were not known during the Vedic period. They may be of later origin and now they assume a lot of importance.

"Lust beclouds a man's heart when it is confused with women's beauty and the mind is dazed. Better far with hot irons bore out both your eyes than encourage in yourselves sensual thought, or look upon a woman's form with lustful desires". (The Buddha). This is a principle in human rights and the police have to respect it.

"Better fall into the fierce tiger's mouth, or under the sharp knife of the executioner, than to dwell with a woman and excite in yourself lustful thoughts....." (The Buddha). In such a noble and divine culture, rape and other obscene acts violating the dignity of woman has no basis or scope. But, instances are not rare that custodial rape and molestation of women in police custody come in the press and media. The Indian mystical thoughts are concerned with timeless mystical knowledge and they always respect women and their sex. The policemen cannot but honour such eternal truths. Earlier, women were not coming to the attention of police, but today more and more women are dealt with by police. Resultingly, a lot is heard of police misbehaviour with women. Some of them violate the inherent dignity of women and in such situations, the police becomes a target of merciless criticism by many including police officers themselves. Policeman is not and cannot be a mechanism of instincts. The values in him must triumph over the animal forces that try to enslave him. The *Bhagavad Gita* wants everyone to raise his self by the self and the policeman is not an exemption to this general rule.

In the United Nations' Convention on the Political Rights of Women [General Assembly Resolution 640 (VII) of 20, December, 1952], it is laid down that "desiring to implement the principle of equality contained in the Charter of the United Nations.

Recognizing that everyone has the right to take part in the government of his country directly and through freely chosen representatives and has the right to equal access to public service in his country, and desiring to equalize the status of men and women in the enjoyment and exercise of political rights in accordance with the provisions of the Charter of the United Nations and of the Universal Declaration of Human Rights,

Having resolved to conclude a Convention for this purpose,

Hereby agree as hereinafter provided,

....

....

Women shall be entitled to hold public offices and to exercise all public functions established by national law on equal terms with men without any discrimination" and accordingly it becomes necessary for more women to be enlisted to police service for maintaining equality between men and women for police work. Nevertheless, the number of women in police service is just a few and logically it means that there is no equality between men and women. Women have to be honoured and the Indian culture does honour women in many ways from time antiquity.

> "Where women are honoured,
> gods are happy. Where
> women are not respected
> all efforts come to
> naught" (Manu).

If Indian mystical revelations are taken in due seriousness, then, necessarily women would be enlisted more in public services. They are honoured and respected everywhere in India as goddess as:

> "Motherliest of mothers, noblest of rivers, godliest of goddesses. O Sarasvati, we are as of no repute, mother, give us high renown" (*Ṛg Veda* 2, 41, 16).

> "Auspicious Mother, goddess who uplifts all, this must be excused by you. A bad son may be born, but there is no bad mother anywhere..... O Ocean of compassion, I think of

> you only when I am immersed in calamities. Do not take it as a roguery on my part. Only when hungry and thirsty, do children think of their mother" (Sankaracharya).

Thus, the mystics have several times and always respected women and placed them at high esteem. A woman is perceived and projected as the mother, sister, goddess and is most respectfully treated in Indian culture. A woman is the symbol of dignity, purity and status. She is eulogized and her role is glorified in many ways. Nevertheless, one may see that there exists gender bias and women are discriminated under several counts. There exists inequality between man and woman. This is certainly not in tune with the revelations of Indian mystical sages. The United Nations want to eradicate this evil and to bring women equal in status with men through their Conventions, Declarations etc. and on a closer scrutiny of them, it may be seen that the world community accepts only those truths which Indian *ṛsis* and sages insisted long-long ago. Sita told Rama: "I shall walk in front of you in the forest ways and tread the thorns and the hard grounds to make them smooth for your feet". This is Indian woman and she is a model to anyone and everyone for all generations. As R.H. Benson said: "There is no limit to the power of a good woman", we may say that women are a force to be reckoned with for ensuring human rights to all in the world.

8

Crime-Doers, Human Rights, Police and Mysticism

Religion considers sin as a violation of its laws and the police consider offences as violations of the penal laws enacted by the State. The society considers all commissions and omissions against all types of laws—social, cultural, ethical, religious, penal, personal, institutional—as crimes. In that sense any wrong-doer is a crime-doer. To quote again—

> "When we men, O Varuna, commit an offence
> before the heavenly host, when we break
> the law through thoughtfulness, have mercy
> on us. Almighty, have mercy on us". (*Ṛg Veda,* 1, 25).

This is how the mystic seers look at wrong-doers. A wrong-doer is not condemned. The Almighty has mercy on them. He forgives them. The United Nations and the World Community too take a considerate and sympathetic view to criminals and wrong-doers. In their Declaration of the Fourth United Nations' Congress on the Prevention of Crime and the Treatment of Offenders, they said:

"Feeling an inescapable obligation to alert the world to the serious consequences for society of the insufficient attention which is now being given to measures of crime prevention, which by definition include the treatment of offenders" and in their declaration, they are very much concerned about the treatment of offenders which include an understanding of crimes and crime-doers. Accordingly, the world community want the people and the police to have recourse to positive methods and procedures for correction and rehabilitation of crime-doers. The Indian mystics had this view and they expressed it in many ways.

"Men in their ignorance sometimes do great evils for the sake of some slight momentary pleasure" (Ramayana) and the society and people become vindictive and retributive in their approach to crime-doers. *An eye for an eye and a tooth for a tooth* principles of criminal justice which was vogue in the past has been rejected by the civilized community today. This might be partly owing to the United Nations' attitude and approach to crime-doers and partly thanks to the mystical teachings from time immemorial. Of course, criminologists and humanitarian penologists have played their role in many ways.

"If a man commits sin, let him not do it again; let him not delight in sin; the accumulation of evil is painful" (*Dhammapada*). The world community is now making attempts to see that man who commits crime (sin) does not repeat it—does not take pleasure in it and for this, many attempts are done world-wide and in all attempts the human dignity and individual's rights are recognized. Every crime-doer has his human rights. The United Nations in their Caracas Declaration (Sixth United Nations' Congress on the Prevention of Crime and the Treatment of Offenders) stated:

> "It is a matter of great importance and priority that programmes for crime prevention and the treatment of offenders should be based on the social, cultural, political and economic circumstances of each country in a climate of freedom and respect for human rights, that Member-States should develop an effective capacity for the formulation and planning of criminal policy, and that all crime-prevention policies should be co-ordinated with strategies for social, economic, political and cultural developments."

From where does the world community get these ideas? No doubt, they come from the inspired truths and revealed teachings.

"O Lord, ... by Thy calm and blissful self which roots out

terror as well as sin, design to make us happy" (*Svetasvatara Upanishad* III, 5). Here the mystical seer wanted to make a happy world—a world wherein all crime prevention strategies were coordinated with strategies for social, economic, political and cultural development.

The United Nations want "to ensure that those responsible for the functioning of the criminal justice system at all levels should be properly qualified for their tasks" (Caracas Declaration) and it refers to police as well. United Nations wish that the functionaries should perform their duties in a "manner which is independent of personal or group interest".

"They who see sin where there is no sin, and see no sin where there is sin, such men embracing false doctrines enter the evil path" (*Dhammapada* 22) and this is what the world community sees in the performance of some functionaries who are not properly qualified for their tasks. Allegations are plenty to show that the police register false cases and what do they achieve by such unjust acts?

"Bad deeds and deeds hurtful to ourselves are easy to do; what is beneficial and good that is very difficult to do" (*Dhammapada*) and the people cannot tolerate such unjust acts. The police cannot keep people in blissful ignorance of what they do.

"Nowhere can any cover up his sin" (*Anguttara Nikaya*) and the police actions, to some extent, are transparent. The police may do many things as they have authority and muscle power. But, just is just and unjust is unjust always and everywhere.

"Strength of body is no protection to the evil-doer" (*Ramayana*) and "when committing a sin, you imagine nobody knows it, but the gods know it, as well as that person who dwells within you" (Vyasa's *Sakuntala*). Police must bear this truth in mind when they perform their duties. That is the reason why it is stated by the United Nations:

> "Criminal policy and administration of justice should be based on principles that will guarantee the equality of everyone before the law without any discrimination, as well

as the effective right of defence and the existence of judicial organs that arc equal to the task of providing speedy and fair justice and of ensuring greater security and protection of the rights and freedoms of all people" (Caracas Declaration).

Milan Plan of Action

Adoption of the Milan Plan of Action took place in the Seventh United Nations' Congress on the Prevention of Crime and Treatment of Offenders. The United Nations stated:

"The success of criminal justice systems and strategies for crime prevention depend on the progress achieved in preserving peace, improving social conditions, making progress towards a new international economic order and enhancing the quality of life". For this, it is necessary that people must desist from committing crimes. Crime, as the United Nations put it, is a major problem of national and, in some cases, international dimensions. In *Katha Upanishad* (II, 24) it is emphatically stated:

"He who has not ceased from bad conduct cannot obtain *Brahma* by *Vidya*" and this is what the United Nations too feel when they say: "Certain forms of crime can hamper the political, economic, social and cultural development of people and threaten human rights, fundamental freedom and peace, stability and security". (Milan Plan of Action).

"He who has no understanding, who is unmindful and impure reaches not the goal" (*Katha Upanishad,* III, 7, 8) and for human development and peace, people must desist from committing crimes.

"The evil-doing, the deluded, the vilest men, they come not to me, they whose wisdom is destroyed by illusion, who have embraced the nature of demons" (*Gita*, VI, 15) and the United Nations repeat the same thing in their Milan Plan of Action.

Guiding Principles for Crime Prevention and Criminal Justice

What are the guiding principles for crime prevention and criminal justice? The principles are well laid down in the mystical writings of Indian sages.

"Hypocrisy, arrogance and conceit, wrath and also harshness and unwisdom are his who is bound, O Partha, with demoniacal properties" (*Gita*, XVI, 4).

"Wrath, desire, avarice, delusion, craving, mercilessness, censoriousness, vanity, grief, attachment, envy, reviling others—these twelve should be avoided by a man of high qualifications" (*Sanatsugatiya,* III). The mystical revelations are more individual centered for prevention of crimes and the United Nations do not see it in the way it must be viewed. The United Nations view:

"Alarmed by the growth and seriousness of crime in many parts of the world, including both conventional and non-conventional criminality which have a negative impact on the quality of life."

Considering that crime, particularly in its new forms and dimensions, seriously impairs the development process of many countries, as well as their international relations, thus, *inter alia,* compromising the attainment of the objectives of the international development strategy for the Third United Nations Development Decade and the establishment of new international economic order.

Noting that the function of the criminal justice system is to contribute to the protection on the basic values and norms of society... This view shows that the United Nations do not give adequate importance to the role of individuals in the prevention of crimes. The mystical seers, on the other hand, emphasize:

> "Boastful, lustful, haughty, irascible, unsteady, one who does not protect (those dependant on him)—these six sinful acts are performed by sinful men who are not afraid even in the midst of great danger. One whose thoughts are all about

> enjoyments, who prospers by injuring (others), who repents of generosity, who is miserly, who is devoid of power (of knowledge), who esteems the group (of senses), who hates his wife... these seven are the seven forms of cruelty"
>
> (*Sanatsugatiya* III).

> "Anger, drunkenness, deception, envy, these constitute uncleanliness". (The Buddha)

The importance of individual in the prevention of crime has always been of paramount importance to Indian mysticism.

"The *Brahman* who has removed all sinfulness who is free from haughtiness, from impurity, who has self-restraint, who is an accomplished master of knowledge, who has fulfilled duties of holiness; such, a *Brahman* justly considers himself a Brahmin" (here means a noble soul and it has no caste significance). This is what Indian philosophy teaches. In the Guiding Principles for Crime Prevention and Criminal Justice in the context of Development and a New International Order, United Nations speak of:

1. International order and relational structures.
2. New International economic order and individual guarantees.
3. Development objectives and elimination of causes of injustice.
4. New directions and approaches.
5. Relations between States.
6. Harmful crimes, industrial crimes, economic crimes, corporate responsibility, victim compensation etc.

It seems that the United Nations, as said earlier, are not individual centered in their approaches. They speak more about international co-operation in crime prevention and criminal justice. They speak about technical co-operation, co-operation among developing countries, regional and international activities etc.

"O effulgent Lord! Destroy our sins and grant us splendour.

Burn our sins" (*Atharva Veda,* 4, 33, 1) and that is the only way the people are able to prevent crimes and establish a new world order—say the sages in Indian mysticism.

Crime-Doers, Human Rights and Police

United Nations have brought out a Code of Conduct for Law Enforcement Officers (16th plenary meeting, 17 December, 1979).

> "Mindful that the nature of the functions of law enforcement in the defence of public order and the manner in which those functions are exercised have a direct impact on the quality of life of individuals as well as of society as a whole.
> "Conscious of the important task which law enforcement officials are performing diligently and with dignity, in compliance with the principles of human rights.
> "Aware, nevertheless, of the potential for abuse which the exercise of such duties entails,
> "Recognizing that the establishment of a code of conduct for law enforcement officials is only one of several important measures for providing the citizenry served by law enforcement officials with protection of all their rights and interests"

This is what the General Assembly says at the beginning of the Code of Conduct for Law Enforcement Officers. In short, the United Nations insist that the law enforcement officers must respect human rights and dignity. In other words, there must not be evil minded people in law enforcement. They must be ethical in their attitude and approaches to crime-doers during law enforcement. Otherwise they will be rejected by the human society as they are wicked people.

"Repel evil-minded persons" (*Yajur Veda,* 19, 38). The law enforcement officers must look at others as friends and not enemies.

"May we all look at each other with a friendly eye!" (*Yajur*

Veda, 36, 18). The law enforcement agencies must be "representative of and responsive and accountable to the community as a whole" and if that is the desire of the international community and of the United Nations, then they must mingle with people and especially with crime-doers in a human rights friendly way. The law enforcement officials must not have enmity or hostility towards law breakers and crime-doers.

> "They alone are the true sons of God, who destroy enmity" (*Rg Veda* 8, 18, 5).

Every criminal is a human person endowed with human dignity. He is the image of God just like any law enforcement official.

> "Bear not enmity to anyone. God is contained in every heart. Enmity and jealousy shall depart from the heart of him, who heareth God's praises" (Bawan Akhare Pauri, 46).

A law enforcement official who does not respect the human rights of others is an enemy to himself and to others. Sri Madhava Deva Nama Ghosa says: "Each man is his own friend; he himself is also his own enemy; he himself destroys and protects himself".

Use of Force by Law Enforcement Officers

Article 3 of the Code of Conduct for Law Enforcement officials reads:

"Law Enforcement officials may use force only when strictly necessary and to the extent required for the performance of their duty". It means that the use of force by police is exceptional. Police can use only reasonable force when they effect or assist in the lawful arrest of offenders or suspected offenders etc. If at all necessary, no force which is disproportionate to the actualisation of the legitimate objective must be used. Use of third degree, calling of epithets by police etc. are human rights violations. Use of firearm is considered as an extreme measure. Use of force in an unreasonable way—in an unjustifiable way—in a human rights unfriendly way—is the expression of frenzy and it has many defects. *Sanatsugatya* V says: (to quote once again).

"Frenzy has eighteen defects.........hatred of men, factitiousness, censoriousness, untruthful speech, lust, wrath, want to control, speaking ill of others, back-biting, mismanagement in business, quarrelsomeness, animosity, troubling living creatures, want of forgiveness, delusion, flippancy, loss of reason. Therefore, a wise man should not be subject to frenzy for it is always censured". The United Nations too speak the same thing. The world community is not at all in favour of a police officer/man inflicting, instigating or tolerating any act of torture or other cruel, inhuman or degrading treatment or punishment" (Article 5 of the Code of Conduct for Law Enforcement officials). There is also another declaration emphasizing the same and it is the "Declaration on the Protection of All Persons from Being Subjected to Torture and Other Cruel, Inhuman or Degrading Treatment or Punishment". Any act of torture is considered as an offence to human dignity.

The Buddha says that "lust and angry passion are the constant miseries of the world" and if that is so, then torture, inhuman, cruel and degrading treatment to any person—no matter, he is a detinue, suspected offender, arrestee—is worse than that and when it comes from a police officer, it deserves to be condemned in strongest words. *Dhammapada* (1, 5) says:

> "Here in this world, anger is never pacified by anger. By non-anger is anger pacified. This is the ancient law"

and it is also the current law adopted and proclaimed by the international community.

The Economic and Social Council (15th plenary meeting, 24 May, 1989) adopted some guidelines for the effective implementation of the Code of Conduct for Law Enforcement officials.

Use of Force and Firearms by Police

The United Nations consider the work of law enforcement officials as social service of great importance. According to the international view, police actions have an ethical basis and precisely, therefore, they have to keep the ethical issues associated with the use of force whenever they interact with people, especially the crime-doers and suspected offenders.

The United Nations say:

"Law enforcement officials, in carrying out their duty, shall, as far as possible, apply non-violent means before resorting to the use of force and firearms. They may use force and firearms only if other means remain ineffective or without any promise of achieving the intended result". There are instances of police officers resorting to violence and to the use of firearms (Blinding episode, custodial violence, rape in police custody, simulated encounters etc.) even when they are not necessary. In order not to become violent, police officers must have self-control.

"Self-controlled man, moving among objects with senses under restraint and free from attractions and aversion attains to tranquillity. In tranquillity, all sorrow is destroyed" (*Gita* II, 64, 65). This is how a police officer must be when he interacts with crime-doers and suspected offenders.

> "In restraining the organs which run wild among ravishing sensualities, a wise man will apply diligent care, like a charioteer in managing restive horses" (*Manava Dharma Sastra*).

The policeman is expected to do it when he manages a law and order situation or when he investigates crimes or dealing with crime-doers. He must apply diligent care and perform his duties in a human rights friendly manner.

The United Nations' Basic Principles on the Use of Force and Firearms by Law Enforcement officials say further:

> "Whenever the lawful use of force and firearms is unavoidable, law enforcement officials shall—

(a) Exercise restraint in such use and act in proportion to the seriousness of the offence and the legitimate objective to be achieved;
(b) Minimize damage and injury, and respect and preserve human life;
(c) Ensure that assistance and medical aid are rendered to any injured or affected persons at the earliest possible moment;
(d) Ensure that relatives or close friends of the injured or affected person are notified at the earliest possible moment."

All these principles are appreciated world-wide and are implemented in many countries. All these principles are seen in ancient Indian literature and mystical revelations. But, they did not or could not attract international attention until, perhaps, the United Nations put the same thing in a more solemn manner.

"Forbearance, control of mind, meditation, austerity, truthfulness, compassion, memory, contentment, charity, indifference from sense pleasures, faith, modesty, kindliness and regard for the soul are the virtues of good men" (*Bhagawata Purana*, 11, 25, 2) and if these qualities are seen in police officers, all of them will be good men. They, then, will exercise restraint in the use of force and they will act only in proportion to the seriousness of the offence and the legitimate objective to be achieved.

"One should first control his mind as mind alone is unconquerable: One can be happy in this world and hereafter only by subduing his mind" (*Uttradhain Sutra* 4, 12). Attempts, therefore, are made so that every policeman/officer attains maximum self control or control of one's mind. Yoga, meditation, introspection etc. are taught in some police training institutions so that police personnel get adequate ego controls in them. India is a free democratic country and the colonial rule came to an end in 1947. The police now are transparent and accountable(?).

"Governments shall ensure that arbitrary or abusive use of

force and firearms by law enforcement officials is punished as a criminal offence under law". Perhaps, the concepts of force, firearms, criminal offence etc. were not very clear to the *ṛsis* when they revealed eternal truths and, therefore, there might not be such words and provisions in the mystical truths. Allegations are heard at times that the police use force and firearms on crime-doers and people. Later, commissions of inquiry are appointed and ultimately, the policeman is blamed. People in such situations express their disliking to police and call the act human right unfriendly. When truth is brought out, people like or dislike the police and their doings.

United Nations' Basic Principles further lay down: "Law enforcement officials shall not use firearms against persons except in self-defence or defence of others against the imminent threat of death or serious injury, to prevent the perpetration of a particularly serious crime involving grave threat to life, to arrest a person presenting such a danger and resisting their authority, or to prevent his or her escape". People in authority or who have authority must use it intelligently with wisdom and prudence.

"A man is not just, if he carries a matter by violence" (*Dhammapada*, 19) and violence against a crime-doer or suspected offender must be justifiable. The law and people will be able to protect police officers only if they are just and honest in using force against anybody including suspects, arrestees, detinues and so on.

> "God protects him, who is just and truthful and destroys him, who is not so" (*Ṛg Veda,* 3, 26, 9).

Policing Persons in Custody or Detention

United Nations say: "Law enforcement officials, in their relations with persons in custody or detention, shall not use force, except when strictly necessary for the maintenance of security and order within the institution or when personal safety is threatened". The principle shows that the police must show respect to all, including those who are in custody or under detention.

"Reverence to the great ones, reverence to the lesser ones. Reverence to the young, reverence to the old" (*Ṛg Veda* 1, 27, 13). This is the mystical revelation and, therefore, showing reverence to detinues means respect for human rights.

Universal Declaration of Human Rights and International Covenants

Earlier, articles contained in the U.D.H.R. and International Covenants relating to the rights of crime-doers and their parallels in Indian mysticism have been brought out. The United Nations' Convention Against Torture and Other Cruel, Inhuman or Degrading Treatment or Punishment also give a lot of insights into the rights of crime-doers. The human rights of the detinues are given in Body of Principles for the Protection of All Persons under any Form of Detention or Imprisonment. There are parallels in mysticism to all which are seen in United Nations' declarations, conventions and documents on human rights and in that way, the parallels in mysticism throw light to the international community as to what to do and how to go about.

"The light which residing in the sun, in the moon, in the fire, illumines the whole world; know that light to be Mine (*Gita* 15, 12) and that is what one may say about human rights and mystical truths. The light which residing in the mystical revelations—inspired truths—illumines the whole world in all things including human rights and dignity of human person. People do not know it, for they are ignorant.

I quote and reiterate here: "As people ignorant of the presence of a golden treasure which has been hidden underground, may walk over it again and again and yet never find it, so all beings though every moment living in *Brahman,* never find Him, for He is hidden by the layer of ignorance" (*Chandogya Upanishad* VIII, 3, 2). Likewise, many people who violate the human rights of people do so because they are ignorant. The United Nations' attempts will make the international community to become aware of the eternal truths which had been in existence in the mystical writings of Indian sages.

9

Victims, Human Rights, Police and Mysticism

Victims, victimology, victim justice, victimogenesis, victim-compensation, etc. are concepts of recent origin. But, they have been in existence from time antiquity and the mystical seers in India had the inspired vision. They never wanted a crime-doer to become a victim of divine displeasure.

"Have mercy on us,
Almighty, have mercy on us" (*Ṛg Veda* 1, 25).

That was how they prayed to God. Repentance for the sins (crimes) one committed and craving for the mercy of God—they could be seen in mystical revelations. Victims of crime, sufferings, injustice, abuse of power and authority approached God for getting consolation and compensation.

"O men! As I (God) have given this word which is the word of salvation for all mankind, namely for the Brahmins, for the Kshatriyas, for the Shudras, for the Vaisyas, for the dependants and even for those who are of low birth, so should you do also" (*Yajur Veda*, 26, 2). "Salvation"—that might be the compensation for the sufferings one had.

> "Yama is not death as some think. He is one that gives bliss to the good and woe to the bad". (*Mahabharata* V, 42, 6).

This was how victim-compensation was ensured.

"May He who confers bliss and wisdom on the devoted, destroying their sins and sorrows and punishing all breakers of law..........endow us with good thoughts" (*Svetasvatara Upanishad,* IV, 12). The one who suffered injustice on earth could get compensation in many ways from the Eternal Tribunal of God who could see the justice and injustice in everything.

United Nations and Victim Justice

Of course, Indian mysticism accepted victim justice in various forms.

> "Where there is happiness and delight, where joy and pleasure reside, where desires of our desire are attained, there make me immortal" (*Ṛg Veda* 9, 113), and

> "The bliss of *Brahman* is not to be considered equal to a result mathematically arrived at by multiplying human joy by many hundred folds, but it is the bliss that is indescribable and infinite" (*Taittiriya Upanishad*).

The world community was not concerned much with the victims of crime/victims of abuse of power and authority till recently. The system was more a criminal centered or criminal oriented. Why think in this way? The Declaration of the *Basic Principles of Justice for Victims of Crime and Abuse of Power* was adopted by the General Assembly (Resolution 40/34) only on 29 November 1985.

Declaration of Basic Principles of Justice for Victims of Crime and Abuse of Power

The General Assembly of the United Nations, in the beginning of the above Declaration writes:

"Cognizant that millions of people throughout the world suffer harm as a result of crime and abuse of power and that the rights of these victims have not been adequately recognized". The world community thus feels that injustice has been done to victims of crimes and victims of the abuse of power/authority. Hence, it is further written:

"Recognizing that the victims of crime and the victims of abuse of power, and also frequently their families, witnesses, and others who aid them are unjustly subjected to loss, damage, or injury and that they may in addition, suffer the hardship when assisting in the prosecution of offenders". The police are blamed by many in victimizing the witnesses, suspects and their families in many ways and the international community is, not at all, favouring such atrocities on human beings and their rights. In the pretext of law enforcement or in enforcing law, the police are not expected to victimize the people.

"The heaven and earth sustain justice by loving man" (*Ṛg Veda* 3, 26, 9) and not at all by victimizing people. One who knows God who is omnipresent—all knowing—cannot harm others—cannot victimize people—cannot injure anyone. This has been the mystical thought.

Who is a victim? This has been defined in the Declaration and it reads:

> "Victims" means persons who, individually or collectively, have suffered harm, including physical or mental injury, emotional suffering, economic loss or substantial impairment of their fundamental rights, through acts or omissions that are in violation of criminal laws operative within Member-States, including those laws prescribing criminal, abuse of power..... The term 'victim' also includes, where appropriate, the immediate family or dependants of the direct victim and persons who have suffered harm in intervening to assist victims in distress or to prevent victimization".

Why do people become victims? Why do they suffer harm? The causes are to be identified before remedies are suggested. One of the main reasons may be lack of respect for others and their rights. People suffer physical or mental injury. They become victims of emotional suffering, economic loss or substantial impairment of their fundamental rights. Man sins against man and sometimes, it is against a man who loves the sinner. This exists everywhere and all throughout human history.

"If we have sinned against the man who loves us, have ever wronged friend or comrade, have ever done an injury to a neighbour who ever dwelt with us or even to a stranger, O Lord! free us from the guilt of this trespass" (*Ṛg Veda* V, 85, 7). This is the mystical teaching and the sages pray to God: "O Lord! free us from the guilt of this trespass". In order to be free from the guilt, one has to compensate the loss sustained by the victim. Just by a prayer, one cannot become free from the guilt. Thus, victim compensation—the concept might be as old as *Ṛg Veda* in Indian mysticism.

"He who regards impartially lovers, friends and foes, strangers, neutrals, foreigners and relatives, also the righteous and unrighteous, excelleth" (*Gita*, VI, 9). This is Indian view and there is no discrimination here. Making victims is not an Indian concept, rather, making people happy is the Indian way of thinking. In *Gita* (III, 20), it is seen:

"..........then having an eye on the welfare of the world also thou shouldst perform action". But, all over the world, people in authority cause loss, damage or injury to others and in law enforcement, many people including witnesses and the families of the crime-doers are unjustly subjected to many losses, damages and injuries. This is the reason why the United Nations have asked the world community "to adopt national and international measures in order to secure universal and effective recognition of, and respect for, the rights of victims of crime and of abuse of power". The international community blames the impure conduct of man against man—the victimizer against the victim and feels that the people must recognize the rights of victims of all descriptions. For this, people have to be pure in their conduct as the mystical sage says:

> "One who is pure in conduct, who is self-restraint and observant of good vows, whose soul is under control, and who is possessed of wisdom, certainly wins success in this world and in the other" (*Mahabharata, Shanti Parva*, 235, 23)

and the inspired truth in Indian mysticism here tells everything about why there are victims in this world. "Without overcoming lust, man cannot hope to rule over self"—says Mahatma Gandhi and if that is the truth, one has to overcome his lust if he wants to recognize and respect the rights of victims of crime and of abuse of power.

Policemen are blamed for their lack of recognition and respect for the rights of the victims of the abuse of power and authority. One of the reasons for it is the lack of control over the self and failure to overcome the lust for power.

> "Right self-control will
> lead a man to heaven;
> the lack of it will lead to
> darkest night" (Tirukkural)

The suspects and offenders have their rights and no police officer has any authority to deny their rights and make them victims of the abuse of power owing to their lust. In cases where the suspects and offenders are made victims of the abuse of power and authority, they are entitled to get victim compensation. United Nations consider such abuse of power as offences under law and make it clear in their Guiding Principles for Crime Prevention and Criminal Justice in the context of Development and a New International Economic Order by emphasising:

"The necessary legislative and other measures should be taken in order to provide the victims of crime with effective means of legal protection, including compensation for damage suffered by them as a result of the crimes". Human Rights Commissions order compensation to all victims of abuse of power and authority by police. Policeman must, therefore, remember:

"He is an ideal man who shows respect to his elders, free from shallowness, deceitfulness, is not disrespectful to anyone in the least, deserts his anger readily, is a true friend and is not proud of his learning, does not talk ill of others, is not angry with friends and praises even a discarded friend in his absence, is not quarrelsome, possessor of wisdom, preserver of vows, ashamed of evil acts, controller of senses and mind" (*Uttradhian Sutra*, 11, 10 to 13). A policeman/officer must have this frame of mind when he deals with suspects and offenders. This attitude alone can reduce victimization of people during crime investigation and law enforcement. The police have to become responsive to what is required of them towards just justice administration. They must observe the Code of Conduct and ethical norms when they interact with suspects and offenders. Secret places of detention and incommunicado detention must be avoided at any cost. Both are victimization in every sense of the word. Only with such attitudes and approaches can the police get satisfaction in their job.

"With imperfections exhausted, doubts dispelled, senses controlled, engaged in the good of all beings, the holy men obtain absolute bliss" (*Gita*, V, 25). All beings include suspects and offenders as well.

"Self-restraint, forgiveness, patience, energy, contentment, truthfulness of speech, modesty, abstention from injury, from the evil practices called *Vyasana,* and cleverness, these are productive of happiness" (*Mahabharata, Shanti Parva*, 291, 19). The police work must produce happiness and victimization has no scope in police job. This is the reason why United Nations say:

"Victims should be treated with compassion and respect for their dignity". The mystical truths affirm that all human beings must be treated with compassion and respect for their dignity.

"He should be patient, forgiving, pure in conduct, severe when occasion requires it, acquainted with the efficacy of exertion, respectful in is his behaviour....ready to do what is just, self-restrained, always sweet-speeched, forgiving unto enemies, practicing charity personally, possessed of faith, of agreeable features, ready to extend the hand of succour to persons plunged in distress,......" (*Mahabharata, Shanti Parva,* 118, 17, 20). What a noble thought and wisdom if the policemen can put it into practice when they deal with suspects, offenders and other human beings! If the policemen are able to do so, there is no need for any guidelines for them to become so.

Universal Declaration of Human Rights and Victimology

Victimology got developed into an independent science only after 1948. At the time when Universal Declaration of Human Rights was enacted by the United Nations in 1948, many including those who drafted the Universal Declaration did not know the implications and relevance of victims' rights, victim compensation, victimology etc. on human rights. This might be the reason why they did not have a place in U.D.H.R. proclaimed on 10 December, 1948. Indian mystical seers, at the same time, spoke about victims and their rights in their own way. In ancient India, the victims' rights and their rights to get compensation were recognized and were allowed when issues and criminal cases were settled at village level. The United Nations' International Covenant on Civil and Political Rights (16 March, 1966), Article 9(5) reads: "Anyone who has been victim of unlawful arrest or detention shall have an enforceable right to compensation". Though the victims' right to compensation was thus recognized in India from time antiquity through her customs and village level practices here, it received legal sanction, first under the law of tort after the British arrival and later by other enactments only recently after India became independent. Of course penal sections for policemen resorting to coercion and third degree are seen in the Indian Penal Code 1860, nevertheless, there was no law specifically intended for claiming compensation for victims of abuse of power/authority by police. After the enactment of the Protection of Human Rights Act—1993, people approach National/States Human Rights Commissions for claiming compensation for the sufferings/ injuries caused to them by abuse of power and authority by police.

> "Given over to egoism, power, insolence,
> lust and wrath, these malicious ones hate
> Me in the bodies of others and I their own" (*Gita*, XVI, 18)

and that is a reason for employing torture on people. The suspects and offenders under law are made victims of abuse of power and authority by police. Egoism, power, insolence, lust and wrath work as powerful forces for victimizing people and in so doing, the law enforcement officers show disrespect to them and to others—to God and his creations which according to mystical revelations is an offence against God and man.

Declaration on the Protection of All Persons from being subjected to Torture and other Cruel, Inhuman or Degrading Treatment or Punishment

The General Assembly of the United Nations adopted the above Declaration on 9th December 1975 [Resolution 3452 (XXX)]. In the said Declaration, United Nations stated categorically that an act of torture or other cruel, inhuman or degrading treatment or punishment was an offence to human dignity. In every sense, it is victimization and doubtlessly, it is a denial of victim justice. Why should a man be victimized? Is there a perfect man in the world? Victimization is as bad as any other crime committed by a criminal. The law enforcement officers here behave just like any other criminals and the United Nations want to stop that. For, the United Nations feel that there is no one who is perfect in the world and precisely, therefore, there is no justification in employing torture on suspects/offenders in law by the law enforcement agency. This is what the Buddha says:

"There is no one in the world who is not blamed". If that is the truth, then what justification has the police have to employ torture on suspects/offenders in law? Hence the United Nations add:

"No State may permit or tolerate torture or other cruel, inhuman or degrading treatment or punishment". History so far may prove that the police have resorted to all sorts of inhuman and degrading treatment to suspects/offenders and some of them were such that only human imagination could conceive of. Why should the law enforcement machinery become so cruel to people? When the law enforcement officers do so they are not fulfilling their social duties.

"They who neglect their social duties for their individual life fall in darkness; and those who sacrifice their individuality for social popularity fall into greater darkness" (*Isha Upanishad*).

Studies show that the police torture suspects to get quick results in no time and thereby they want to increase their popularity and certainly, *they fall into greater darkness,* as the *Upanishad* warns all of us. Against the use of torture and degrading treatment, the United Nations insist that each State "shall keep under systematic review interrogation methods and practices as well as arrangements for the custody and treatment of persons deprived of their liberty". The United Nations say further:

"Where it is proved that an act of torture or other cruel, inhuman or degrading treatment or punishment has been committed by or at the instigation of a public official, the victim shall be afforded redress and compensation in accordance with national law". There must be the purity of conduct in all actions by anybody including police officials and public servants. If there is no purity of conduct, then the victim must get compensation. This is the world-view as it is seen in the United Nations' Declaration.

> "Purity of conduct beareth virtue as its fruit.
> Purity of conduct beareth wealth as its fruit.
> It is purity of conduct that bringeth on prosperity.
> And it is purity of conduct that driveth away
> all inauspicious indications".
>
> (*Mahabharata, Udyoga Parva,* Sec. 112).

The Declaration of the United Nations once again reminds the public officials to do only the right things during law enforcement.

"Follow the right life. Do not follow the evil way. The righteous man rests happily in this world and in the next" (*Dhammapada* 13, 13). This is the reward which righteous people get when they do the right things in the right way. Justice must be administered in a right way.

Convention against Torture and other Cruel, Inhuman or Degrading Treatment or Punishment

In the above Convention, the rights of the victims has been

accepted and proclaimed. The Convention reads:

"Each State Party shall ensure in its legal system that the victim of an act of torture obtains redness and has an enforceable right to fair and adequate compensation, including the means for as full rehabilitation as possible. In the event of the death of the victim as a result of an act of torture, his dependants shall be entitled to compensation". The victims' rights are emphasized here. The law enforcement officers must, first of all, respect the law before they insist others to respect the law. The uniform they wear and the authority they possess are not licences to do anything they want. They have to respect the dignity of man and torturing the suspects and offenders in law is not law enforcement. The mind of the law enforcement officer must be pure if he wants to administer just justice.

> "A man is not a supporter of the law because
> he talks too much........ he is the supporter
> of the law, who never neglects the law". (*Dhammapada*).

This must be the attitude of police when they interrogate suspects or offenders in law. He must not neglect the law and the law is that he should not use torture when he enforces law.

In the Body of Principles for the Protection of All Persons Under Any Form of Detention or Imprisonment, the United Nations state under Principle 15:

> "Damage incurred because of acts or omissions by a public official contrary to the rights contained in these principles shall be compensated according to applicable rules on liability provided by domestic law".

Can compensation in terms of money for the damages/loss caused to the victims of crime/abuse of power or authority be sufficient? Everything compensated in terms of money is an approach in the modern world. The mystics do not feel so. They say:

"Lo verily, not for love of wealth is wealth dear, but for the love of the *Atman* wealth is dear" (*Brihadaranyaka Upanishad*

II, 4, 1, 5) and the current thinking that money compensates/can compensate all damages caused to the victims of crime/abuse of power or authority does not seem to appeal the mystical saints. Money may give some relief in the material world, but can no way be a compensation to the loss caused to the victims of crime/abuse of power and authority. With money alone one cannot become happy. And in *Adi Parva* (75, 49), it is written: "The desire for happiness does not cease by the enjoyment of pleasures". But, in all Conventions and Declarations of the United Nations, one may see that the world community talks of compensation in terms of money and happiness derived through wealth. But see how the mystics view it: "The silkworm dies of its wealth" (*Mahabharata,* 12, 330, 29). There is an eternal reality. The reality is above money-considerations. A man can not victimize another man if he thinks that the "Lord dwelleth in the hearts of all beings" (*Gita* XVIII, 61) and that is the lesson taught to people by the mystical sages. In order not to become a victimizer, "purge your body, speech and mind from all sins" (*Yajur Veda,* 35, 11). And to conclude: "May we like the sun and moon tread on the straight, righteous and fixed path. May we help each other by knowing each other, without causing injury" (*Ṛg Veda,* 5, 51, 15).

10

Equal Justice, Human Rights, Police and Mysticism

Equal justice is different from equality before law and equal protection under law. Equal justice, in general terms, means justice to all—to the crime-doer, to the victim, to the society and to the justice system. In fact, the United Nations are at it although they speak of criminal justice, juvenile justice, victim justice, gender justice, social justice etc. The mystical sages could see such an equal justice then and they found that everyone got his due from "THEE".

> "I see Thee without beginning, middle or end, infinite in power, of manifold arms, the sun and the moon Thine eyes, the burning fire Thy mount; heating the whole universe with Thy radiance. The space betwixt heaven and earth and all the quarters are filled by the Thee alone" (*Gita*, XI, 19, 20).

This is equal justice because the "space betwixt heaven and earth and all the quarters are filled with Thee alone" and in such a situation, everyone will get his due justice. The crime-doer, the victim, the society will get justice in the proper way.

"His infinite mercy is open to everyone" (Vivekananda) and certainly, there one finds equal justice.

United Nations and Equal Justice

United Nations have brought out many types of justices in their various Declarations and Conventions and all these justices are seen in some form or another in Indian mystical revelations. Human justice—that is what the United Nations want. Man administers justice to man and how it is and it must be? This is what the United Nations are concerned with. But, the *ṛsis* of the Indian mysticism speak about divine justice and certainly, it will be superior to all kinds of justices of which man may conceive.

"Deal not unjustly with others, and you shall not be dealt with unjustly"—this means that there is a greater justice over the justice which man administers on earth. The Eternal Tribunal of God—that is there above all man-made tribunals. In *Rg Veda* 9, (10, 14, 2), "One sees that Yama, the god of death and judgement, knows all about us."

"In the next world, they place good and evil deeds in a balance. Whichever of the two shall outweigh the other, that he shall follow, whether it is good or evil. Now whosoever knows this places himself in the balance in this world and is freed from being weighed in the next world, it is by good deeds and not by bad, that his scale outweighs" (*Satapatha Brahmana* XI, 2, 7, 33). The Indian saints believe that justice will be done and no one can escape from being judged good or bad. This sort of approach has great impact upon individuals. Everyone will be administered justice and the mystics say:

"Yama is not death as some think. He is one that gives bliss to the good and woe to the bad" (*Mahabharata,* V, 42, 6). Hence the *ṛsis* say that man must be good. And the United Nations add that ever human being has fundamental human rights. His dignity and worth of the human person must be recognized. Man and woman have equal rights. All these facts are to be accepted as they only will promote social progress and better standards of life. This is what the mystics too say and they say in simple language that man must be good. "A calf can find its mother cow among a thousand kines; so good and evil done returns and whispers *I am thine"—Panchatantra*. An unjsut man will have problems and aches and history proves that "disregard and contempt for human rights have resulted in barbarous acts which have outraged the conscience of mankind" (U.D.H.R., UNO).

United Nations, Mysticism, Equal Justice and Human Rights

As pointed out earlier, the United Nations do not speak of equal justice. They speak of criminal justice, human rights justice, victim justice etc. and not of equal justice. About criminal justice, the United Nations under Article 11, U.D.H.R. lay down:

"Everyone charged with a penal offence has the right to be presumed innocent until proved guilty according to law in a public trial at which he has had all the guarantees necessary for his defence". Why should one presume that a *guilty is innocent* until he is proved guilty? Why cannot he think that he may or may not have committed the offence and let him prove his position. In an equal justice system, both the prosecution and the defence must get justice and the view of the world community is in favour of the accused and the mystical sages may disagree with the approach of the United Nations. The sinner has to repent and he cannot take a position that he has not committed the offence. No presumption of innocence will be there in favour of him.

"Whatever sin, O God, we have committed against Thee, in thoughtfulness, men as we are make Thou as sinless before Aditi" (*Ṛg Veda*, 4, 12, 4).

"Absolve us from the sins of our fathers and from those which we have committed with our own bodies" (*Atharva Veda* 4, 16, 15). In every sense, this is a better approach than what is seen in the United Nations' approach in the U.D.H.R. Why should the crime-doer/offender in law be given a preferred treatment? The preferred treatment given to the crime-doer is doubtlessly an injustice done to the victim of offence and to the society. It is against the principles of equal justice under law.

"Verily, that which is justice is truth" (*Brihadaranyaka Upanishad*, 1, 4, 14) and if so, doing injustice to the victim and to the society by presuming that the crime-doer (accused) is innocent will be against truth. Whatever one may speak about human rights—about accused's rights—about presumption of innocence—there is some truth in everything and that truth alone is justice and the mystical sages accept such truths only as justice and nothing more.

What is the role of police in administration of justice at present? If every person charged with a penal offence is presumed to be innocent as per U.D.H.R., then how can the police deal with him prior to his trial before a court of law? Police can deal with him only with suspicion—strong suspicion—stronger suspicion—suspicion rebutted—suspicion removed with proof—positive proof to prove that he is the crime-doer. Once the police do so, again he is presumed to be innocent under the human rights laws. This is ununderstandable and the view now is to approach the issue without forming any presumptions in favour or against anybody on the prosecution or defence side. *Noquisitorial system* of administration of justice may ensure equal justice in a meaningful manner.

Equal Justice and Indian Constitution

"We, the people of India having solemnly resolved to constitute India into a sovereign democratic Republic and to secure to all its citizens justice, social, economic and political, liberty of thought, expression, belief, faith and worship, equality of status and opportunity........" (The Preamble of the Constitution of India) and it shows how much are the Indians concerned with human rights, dignity, equality and equal justice under law. The founding fathers of the Indian Constitution have been certainly moved by the teachings and visions of Indian mystical sages when they drafted our Constitution. For, they wanted equal justice to all and I do not feel that the United Nations think in this direction when they speak of criminal justice, victim justice, juvenile justice etc. in an individualistic way.

God administers equal justice to all—in other words, he is just to all equally. He gives air, water, rain, heat to all alike and He does not make any distinctions among the people.

"I am the soul of all beings, am always present in all beings" (*Srimad Bhagavata*) and if that is the mystical revelation, then everybody is equal to anybody and in everybody the presence of God is found. In such a situation, Article 6 of the U.D.H.R.: *Everyone has the right to recognition everywhere as a person before law*—does not make any sense. For, the mystical truth is that "*I am the soul of all beings*" and if that is so, there is no question of not recognizing everyone as a person before law. "I am there in everyone" and "I am there in the law enforcer and in the law violator". Policemen as enforcers of law cannot deal with people discriminately. Any policeman who employs torture on a suspect or treating people in a cruel, inhuman or degrading manner does so with God, Almighty. Policeman may be able to convince people saying that he is administering just justice or equal justice. But, he cannot fool the Almighty. "The *Purusha* is of a thousand eyes (omniscient), a thousand feet (omnipresent) .... He is also the master of Immortality"

(*Ṛg Veda,* 10, 90, 1-3).

Policeman must administer *equal justice* to the crime-doer, to the victim of offence, to the victim of abuse of power/misuse of authority, to the society and to the justice system itself. For, Article 7, U.D.H.R. reads that "all are equal before the law and are entitled without any discrimination to equal protection of the law". The revealed truths are much more than what is accepted by the United Nations. They explain why all are equal before law. It is not only because man has human rights that everyone is treated as equal before law, but because, all are the children of the same father.

Why must the world community insist that the human rights of people must be recognized? In *Katha Upanishad* (2, 18), one reads:

"Concentrating the mind on the spirit within, man should realize the divine character of his own soul and its inherent freedom. The spirit lodged within oneself is unperceived because of the perplexities of joy and grief and attachments to worldly objects". The reason is very clear here and that is: "man is not able to realize the divine character of his own soul and its inherent freedom". Everybody has a soul having the same divine character and inherent freedom and the people must recognize this fact. In equal justice system, the sublimity of human person in every individual is fully recognized and everyone is given justice due to him. The crime-doer gets his due, the suspect gets his due. The victim gets his due and the society gets its due. The witnesses get their dues and the complainants get their dues. The justice system itself gets its due and it is the precise reason why equal justice system is otherwise called the distributive system of justice. It is alleged that the United Nations do not see distributive justice—Equal Justice—when they deal with human rights. United Nations trust member-States to enforce the international laws on human rights. But the mystical seers do not think that man can do these things alone.

"However much you may try, without God's grace nothing can be achieved"—and this is what the inspired truth tells us. The *mistakes* people committed yesterday might become precedents today and will turn out to be a custom tomorrow. That is what has happened now. Article 11, U.D.H.R. says:

"Everyone charged with a penal offence has the right to be presumed innocent until proved guilty according to law in a public trial at which he has had all the guarantees necessary for his defence". What does it mean? The questions that need answers are—

1. How can one presume that a guilty man is innocent? Presumption is one thing and reality may be another thing.
2. A wrong presumption will necessarily take anyone to wrong conclusions. A guilty person does not have or ought not to have any right to be presumed as innocent. He is guilty and he must be treated as he is. Since it may be difficult to see a guilty man to be innocent or an innocent man to be guilty, it is better to take a *"via media"* position—*i.e.,* he may or may not be innocent. The position can be confirmed on the basis of the proof the prosecution/defence may advance.
3. In the case of an innocent man, there is no need to presume that he is innocent. He is innocent and as such, the question of presumption does not arise. The *Human Rights Law* must be that no innocent man must be brought to trial.

4. Presumption of innocence in favour of the accused means that the system does not trust the system itself. The system believes that the system brings innocent people too for trial and the law takes precautions against such malpractices. What type of human rights justice is it to do so? In such instances, every accused becomes a victim of abuse of power and misuse of authority. This is miscarriage of justice.
5. United Nations talk a lot about torture, arbitrary arrest, unnecessary detention etc. prior to the trial of a person. If the presumption of one's innocence is a human right at the beginning of a trial, then what justification is there to put an innocent man into trouble prior to his trial? If arrest, detention, remand etc. are justified during the pre-trial procedures, then they continue to be justified afterwards and during the trial. If, at the trial, an accused has a right to be presumed innocent, then he has/ought to have a right to be presumed innocent even before it during the pre-trial procedures as well.
6. What justification does a court have to detain an accused in judicial custody if it presumes that he is innocent at the trial stage? What does the court do when he is acquitted as proved innocent? The court detains him in judicial remand and does not award any compensation when he is acquitted as found innocent. Jumping from guilty to innocence and from innocence to guilty and thus a drama may go on, but the procedure does not ensure just justice or equal justice.

There is a story of a sane person made insane by his family and doctors working in the mental hospital. He was forcefully brought to the mental asylum and the influential family members pressured the doctors to *presume* that he was mentally an insane person. The doctors could not presume him in that way, but they had to. As a result, he was administered medicine which was usually given to mental patients. At last, they could make him a mental patient. This is what happens in the case of innocent people who are brought to courts. The innocent people are presumed to be innocent first by the court and they are tried just like guilty people are tried. Instances are plenty to show that some innocent people are punished by the court—just like sane people are made insane by the doctors and family members. Take another example. An insane person was brought to a mental hospital. The doctors presumed him to be sane and they had no medicine to treat sane people. As he was sane, no medicine could be administered to him presuming him to be insane. It is almost like this what is happening in courts of law. Guilty people are brought to the court and the court presumes him to be innocent. The court has no option to try him with a procedure which is applicable to guilty people. The same procedure which is available with the court is followed both in the case of innocent people and in the case of guilty people. The impact is that sometimes, the innocent people are convicted and the guilty are acquitted. The defect lies in the "wrong presumption" formed at the trial stage and the "same procedure" followed in the case of *de facto guilty* and *de facto innocent* people. The United Nations repeat under Article 14(2) of the International Covenant on Civil and Political Rights that—

> "Everyone charged with a criminal offence shall have the right to be presumed innocent until proved guilty according to law".

The human rights law here presumes that the sub-system which brings offenders to court brings innocent people too for trial and the courts of law just *presume* their innocence and proceed further. The courts do not look at the sub-system which brings innocent people before them as evil-doers. This is wrong and is against the mystical teachings.

"These haters, evil, pitiless, vilest among them in the world, I ever throw down into demoniacal wombs—attaining not to me" (*Gita*, XVI, 20-21).

"The evil doing, the deluded, the vilest men, they come not to Me, they whose wisdom is destroyed by illusion, who had embraced the nature of demons" (*Gita,* VII, 15). In fact, this is what the unscrupulous police officers and prosecutors do when they bring innocent people before the courts of law. They are evil-doers and they *"Come not to Me"*.

"Bewildered by numerous thoughts, enmeshed in the web of delusion, addicted to the gratification of desire, they fall downwards into a foul hell" (*Gita*, XVI, 16). Such police functionaries and prosecutors are not aiding administration of justice. And, any amount of *presumption* in favour of such *"innocent accused"* cannot do justice to the victims of abuse of power and misuse of authority. It seems that the United Nations do not take these facts into serious consideration. Perhaps, they think that the Universal Declaration of Human Rights proclaimed about half a century ago does not require any amendments.

Human Rights and Equal Justice

First of all, the United Nations must accept the reality that Human Rights have meaning only if they ensure "Equal Justice" to all who are denied of justice. Human rights justice and equal justice are the two sides of the same coin and one does not have an existence without the other.

Example

On the basis of the presumption of innocence, a guilty escapes punishment. What type of justice does this presumption guarantee? It does not administer justice to the offender, to the victim, to the society and to the justice system itself.

"Shall Presume" and "May Presume"—these are two expressions seen in the evidence laws in criminal trials. The U.D.H.R. and the International Covenant on Civil and Political Rights—both make the presumptions as human rights and precisely, therefore, the expression has the meaning of *"Shall Presume"*. How can such a "SHALL" ensure equal justice which is on the other side of the human rights justice? This is a problem to which the United Nations do not offer any solutions. Human rights justice is intended to guarantee harmony and happiness as

Vyasa rightly says:

"May all beings be happy; may all attain the bliss, may all see happy days". This is not possible with the "Presumption" which the U.D.H.R. and I.C.C.P.R. have.

The concept of Equal Justice is of recent origin and was not known to the United Nations either when they proclaimed the U.D.H.R. or when they declared the International Covenants. Of course, the one who reads all human rights Declarations and Conventions may understand that the United Nations move towards an Equal Justice System which honours human rights justice as well. The millennium, it is hoped, will bring all *justices* under an Equal Justice System.

"Truth alone triumphs and not untruth".

(*Mundaka Upanishad* II, 16)

and that mystical truth affirms that the United Nations cannot but move towards Equal Justice which alone is the truth in the ultimate analysis.

"Verily, that which is justice is truth" (*Brihadaranyaka Upanishad,* 1, 4, 14) and certainly, equal justice alone is truth for the humanity—and that alone is justice for all. All Rights For All and it is for Equal Justice For All.

11

Hindu Dharma, Police, United Nations and Human Rights

Human rights must be respected, ensured and enforced. The United Nations' objective is to see that they are honoured everywhere. In all their Declarations and Conventions, the United Nations repeatedly state: "Whereas the people of the United Nations have in the Charter reaffirmed their faith in fundamental human rights, in the dignity and worth of human person and in the equal right of man and woman and have determined to promote social progress and better standards of life in larger freedom" (U.D.H.R.) and the Hindu mystical view too was exactly the same. Hindu mystical revelation is that God is more fully revealed in many than in the lower creatures. If that is the truth then every man has all rights which any other man enjoys in the world.

"Thou transcendest heaven and earth" (*Ṛg Veda,* 9, 86, 29). For God, there are no boundaries, no distinctions, no castes, no colours, no creeds and, therefore, everybody is equal to anybody. No one can enjoy so many rights as he thinks that he has and no one can deny so many rights to others as he thinks that he can deny. There must be mutual recognition and it comes because the Hindus believe: "I am always present in all beings" (*Srimad Bhagavata*) and, therefore, "All Rights are for All" in the world and here "*Rights*" mean "Human Rights".

'*dhṛ*', the root of *Dharma* in Hinduism means *'to hold'*. Human rights hold the people together and every individual has his '*dharma*'. *Dharma* is virtue and *Adharma* is vice. *Adharma* is disharmony with truth and wherever *adharma* is seen there is violation of human rights. Every man has a desire for the common good and necessarily a desire for respecting human rights. United Nations want this desire to be actualised. The U.N. Declarations and Conventions speak out the *dharma*—the righteousness and they want to hold the people together by mutual respect of human rights.

Abuse of power and misuse of authority is *adharma* and necessarily a human rights violation. Hence, a number of *articles* are provided in their Declarations and Conventions for ensuring the protection of human rights by law enforcement officers and particularly, the police. People have a craving for power and authority. Police officers have power and authority and there is a human urge to misuse the authority and abuse the power. This urge has to be checked. Unless the police control this urge, they cannot protect human rights. For most policemen, power and authority may be a way to express their *'adharma'*. Authority must be exercised in ways of righteousness (*dharma*). For this, they have to blind their will in tune with the international thinking on righteousness (*dharma*). Hindu *dharma* teaches that man does not live by authority alone. Authority alone does not and cannot give human satisfaction. If authority is exercised with *'dharma'*, righteousness, then it gives ultimate satisfaction to people.

Indian mysticism recognises different pathways to exercise one's authority. They are *"jnana"* (wisdom), *'bhakti'* (devotion) and '*karma*' (service). It goes without saying that police must have *jnana, bhakti* and *karma* if they want to be human rights friendly. *Jnana* (wisdom) means a true insight into what they do. In other words, do everything respecting truth and if they do so, it will be human rights friendly. Right actions will take care of themselves.

> "All gifts, the gift of truth excels;
> All tastes, the tastes of Truth excels;
> All joys, the joy of Truth excels. (*Dhammapada*, 24, 21)

Do all the duties with *bhakti* (devotion) and *karma* (service). It means *jnana* plus *bhakti* plus *karma* ensure human rights, justice and *dharma* in the world. The attempts of the United Nations is to weld together the *jnana, bhakti* and *karma* of individuals and nations and that is what is seen in the U.D.H.R.: "Whereas, it is essential to promote the development of friendly relations between nations".

Casteism, *Dharma* and Human Rights

India is a caste-ridden society and in such a society, human rights may be a concept that is decided by the caste—say some critics. Scholars in Indian mysticism attack this view and add that casteism is the result of Indian tolerance and trust. The mystical seers wanted collaboration of races and co-operation of cultures through casteism. Dr. S. Radhakrishnan writes: "Though it has (*caste*) now degenerated into an instrument of oppression and intolerance, though it tends to perpetuate inequality and develop the spirit of exclusiveness, these unfortunate effects are not the central motives of the system". Of course, discrimination on the basis of caste resulted in India and there was social agitation against casteism in the country. The United Nations in U.D.H.R. state: "Every one is entitled to all rights and freedoms set forth in this Declaration, without distinction of any kind, such as race, colour, sex, language, religion, political or other opinion, national or social origin, property, birth or other status". Discrimination on the basis of casteism is not encouraged by the mystical thinkers too. Of course, one may see lower and higher castes in India now. To quote Dr. Radhakrishnan once again: "what we regard as the lower castes have their own taboos and customs, laws and beliefs which they have created for themselves in the course of ages—caste is really custom. Crude and false as the customs and beliefs of others may seem to us, we cannot deny that they help the community adopting them to live at peace itself and in harmony with others. It is a point of social honour for every member to marry within his own caste....The functions of the different castes were regarded as equally important to the well-being of the whole. The screnity of the teacher, the heroism of the warrior, the honesty of the businessman, and the patience and energy of the worker all contribute to the social growth. Each has its own perfection".

Nevertheless, contrary to the mystical teachings, deterioration took place in the concept of casteism and thus the history proved that the caste itself became (becomes) a source of human rights violations in India. Certainly, it was against the *dharma* preached by the mystics. Among the various castes in India, *Kshatriyas*, a group meant to use force, was one. People saw aggressiveness in them and they expressed it on other fellow beings. *Kshatriyas* could control and check the anti-social elements. Thus, they were to police the people. Until organized policing in India came into being, the *Khsatriyas* could render a lot of service to maintain human rights and social harmony. All men were equal in status, the mystics said and "one becomes a Brahmin by his deeds not by his family or birth; even a *Candala* is a Brahmin if he is of pure character' (*Bhagavata*). So far as the attainment of perfection is concerned, even the low castes can attain as much as the high—said Bhagavan Krishna in the Bhagavad Gita. Sri Krishna said: "Those who take refuge in me even of inferior birth, women and *Shudras,* they also attain the highest state and this is what is seen in the movement of human rights all over the world. The mystics could see everything in their divine vision.

Dharmasastra and Human Rights

'*Dharma'* signifies the eternal laws which maintain the universe. It protects everything and means the obligation which everyone has towards other fellow beings. The human rights Declarations of the United Nations too proclaim the same thing in a louder voice. But, a few of the human rights already proclaimed by the United Nations require changes/amendments now as they are not considered/cannot be considered as human rights. For example, today the United Nations favour the accusatorial system of criminal justice administration. Nevertheless, there is a move to accept an equal justice system in a *noquisitorial model.* If that comes into being, some of the human rights which are accepted as human rights may be changed/amended. *Dharmasastra* is not like that. It has its origin in the divine inspiration and it draws its authority from the eternal law which is the *Veda*. Hence, it is immutable. Human rights laws may be changed, but the mystical laws inspired by God cannot be changed by man. They are eternal and absolute. They move from eternity to eternity.

Enforcement of Human Rights Laws and *Dharma*

Kingship is considered as a *conditio sine qua non* for the maintenance of social order. The social order is established by the Creator and it is for the welfare and good of His creatures. People who are ignorant of their duties and responsibilities with other fellow beings are to be caught and controlled by the king. Indian mystics believed that owing to society's degeneration, men lost the inborn sense of their duties. Disorder came into being and the *strong oppressed the weak* and there began human rights violations. Hence the mystical sages said:

> "A society without a king (*a-rajaka*) is not viable. It is the logic of the fish (*i.e.*, the law of the jungle) which is law".

This mystical revelation is followed everywhere and the United Nations in all their Declarations and Conventions say: "State Parties shall" and it means that the State Parties perform the duties of the king. The *Optional Protocol* to human rights laws may contain the words: "calls upon all governments in a position to do so to consider signing and ratifying or acceding to....." and thereafter it becomes the *dharma* of all State Parties to enforce the human rights laws. The *Mahabharata* says that all *dharmas* are comprised in the *raja-dharma* and it means that the king in power or the government in power is to execute human rights law. The police form a part of the executive organ of the government in power and therefore, it goes without saying that protection of human rights becomes a part of the *police-dharma* in any country today. The mystics believed that the functions of the king had a divine nature and in the present set-up, we may say that the *police-dharma* has a divine nature. But how many policemen accept or can accept the divine nature of police job?

How many policemen perform their jobs as a part of *police-dharma?*

Why must the police protect the human rights? Though a direct answer to this question may not be seen in the mystical writings, one may certainly see a number of reasons why the king was to enforce justice to people and to protect their interest. The king today means the government in power. The reasons are—

1. People pay taxes (*bali*) to the king (government) as if it were a salary (*vetana*) given to the king in return for his performing the duty. It includes protection of human rights as well in the modern concepts.
2. There exists a sort of contractual or a quasi-contractual nature between the people and the king (government) following the principle of equity that *ubi emolumentum ibi onus—i.e.,* the liability follows the consideration.
3. The king (government) has a duty to protect his subjects including those who do not pay taxes or are exempted from payment of taxes because of their status, age, infirmities or want of resources.

The *Dharmasastra* emphatically says that a king who fails to protect his subjects loses his subjects' affection and, therefore, it is to the interest of the king himself to see that the rights of the people are protected. The United Nations too say the same thing to all member-States and insist the human rights to be protected. Each State Party tells its police functionaries to protect the rights of the people. The police functionaries who fail to perform their *dharma* fail to fulfil their obligations to the people. The mystics say that the king can punish his subjects and the punishment—*Danda*—is to keep all men on the path of duty. The object of *Danda* is to enable the king to perform his functions. Thus, *Danda* in Indian mysticism is identified with *Dharma* and if *Danda* is not properly and justly administered, it turns against him and brings his ruin. This is what is said in the modern human rights law. The police who are empowered to protect human rights and to see that violators of law are brought to justice cannot but act honestly, fairly and justly.

"Anyone who has been a victim of unlawful arrest or detention shall have an enforceable right to compensation" [Article 9(5), I.C.C.P.R.]

"Each State Party shall ensure in its legal system that the victim of an act of torture obtains redress and has an enforceable right to fair and adequate compensation, including the means for as full rehabilitation as possible. In the event of the death of the victim as a result of an act of torture, his dependants shall be entitled to compensation" (Article 14, Convention against Torture and Other Cruel, Inhuman or Degrading Treatment or Punishment).

These principles of victimology which the United Nations accepted just recently were already recognized in Indian mysticism. In fact, the victimology is as old as Indian mysticism. The inspired truth is that the king can incur no impurity when he is inflicting *Danda.* Kings are bound by vow to administer pure justice. The policemen too are like a king and they should be pure when they execute the law.

"*Dharma* is the sovereignty of sovereignty'.

(*Ksatrasya ksatram yad dharmah*). According to the mystical teachings, the king too must suffer the consequences of his action just like the United Nations say that the State Parties must suffer the consequences of their action whenever human rights are violated by the agencies representing the State.

In Indian mysticism, the most modern concepts of criminal justice, victim justice, gender justice, equal justice etc. are seen.. Human rights justice, social justice, enforcement justice, total justice, just justice too are discussed. But, of course, they are not discussed as they are discussed now and here. The king (*i.e.,* the State) is to protect the subjects against all injustices and that was the revealed truth. The protection has many aspects and they are:

1. The sinner must expiate his sins. For this he must do penance. If he does not do so, he will suffer the fatal consequences which his unexpiated sins will bring on

him. The king must see that the sinner expiates and undertakes penance. He must warn his subjects against committing sins. This is his *dharma.* For expiation and atonement, one sees prisons and penitentiaries today. Simple or rigorous imprisonment may be awarded depending upon the seriousness of the offence. However, human rights laws insist that "no one shall be subjected to cruel, inhuman or degrading treatment or punishment" (Article 5, U.D.H.R.). The mystical seers too say the same thing and remind the kings that the purpose of punishment is expiation from sins—is to save the sinner from the fatal consequences of sins. The modern theory of "correction" has, thus, its roots in the mystical revelations of the Indian sages. In fact, the Standard Minimum Rules for the Treatment of Prisoners, United Nations' Standard Minimum Rules for the Non-custodial Measures (The Tokyo Rules), United Nations' Standard Minimum Rules for the Administration of Justice etc. have their roots in the mystical teachings regarding the purpose of punishment and the *dharma* of kings.

2. The king has the *dharma* to legislate and the purpose here is to make the people respect the rules of conduct prescribed in the *sastras* and to abide by the divine laws. The United Nations too ask the State Parties to fulfil their *dharma* by enacting appropriate legislations for ensuring human rights. The Indian mystics say that every individual has a duty to ensure that he lives according to divine laws (which include the human rights laws today) and he cannot forget his duty or neglect it. If one does so, he may have to face grave peril. The United Nations too say the same thing when they state: "*Whereas it is essential if man is not to be compelled to have recourse, as a last resort, to rebellion against tyranny and oppression, that human rights should be protected by the rule of law*".
3. The mystics say that the king has the *dharma* to see that all those who are the cause of disturbance by their

> reprehensible activities are discouraged and forces eliminated. This is necessary for establishing peace and order. The king's *dharma consciousness,* is the subjects' surety on this. In human rights laws too, the world community places their trust on the State parties and the people.

During the period of mysticism, there were no Human Rights Courts or Human Rights Commissions. But, the mystics insisted that the *sastras* ought to act as supreme arbitrator in disputes relating to law violations. Today, there are international laws regarding human rights and there exist State, National and International Human Rights Commissions and Courts to decide on the issues.

Dharma in Indian mysticism is what is firm and durable. *Dharma* sustains and contains everything and everybody. Hence, no one can be human rights friendly unless he is *dharma*-conscious in life. In order to make the State parties and the people of the world of their *dharma*—to make them *dharma conscious*—the United Nations from time to time proclaim the laws as common standards for their effective recognition and observance by the world community.

Ṛta and Human Rights

The mystics saw *Ṛta —i.e.,* a universal harmony which determines the course of all existence in the world. The mystical seers found the universe as an ordered whole and behind the diversities they perceived a harmonious unity, the *Ṛta*. The United Nations find a harmonious unity—a *Ṛta* —in the world among the people of diversities and they want to get a consensus from all people for the protection of human rights for establishing the *Ṛta* in the world. *Ṛta* thus is a force that keeps up the world together. The word '*Ṛta*' etimologically comes from Sanskrit roort '*ṛ* which means "to go, to move" etc. and it further means to "go in harmony", "to move in peace" and certainly, we require respect for human rights—as the United Nations say—for moving together. '*Ṛta*' is the '*ordering principle'* of the Universe and the fundamental norm of all human behaviour. One may add that the human rights laws are the 'ordering principles' of the universe and the '*basic norms'* of all human behaviour.

The succession of the seasons, the cycles of birth, the alteration of day and night, the growth and decay etc. proceed from *Ṛta*. It causes the universe to run smoothly and guides the universe from its emergence to its decay/dissolution. *Ṛta* controls the cosmic order. *Ṛta*, according to mystical seers, is the foundation of social organization and the fundamental or basic norm of human behaviour. In that sense, the human rights laws are the *Ṛta*, the controlling principles and basic norms of human behaviour. In *Ṛg Veda,* one sees:

> "Sweetly blows the breeze for one who lives according to *ṛta*; rivers flow with sweetness for him"
>
> (*Ṛg Veda*, 1, 105, 12)

and to it one may add: *"sweetly blows the breeze for one who lives according to human rights laws".* For, the peace and harmony of the people (*ṛta*) are decided on the basis and intensity of the respect shown to human rights and human rights principles. These actions in accord with the human rights principles (Human rights may be represented as *ḥr*)—in accord with the *ṛta*—are right. Conversely enough, those which are opposed to *ḥr* (*ṛta*) are bad/wrong. The mystical seers say that anything violating the *ṛta* will cause *anṛta* and *anṛta* will certainly bring in disintegration both in the cosmic and psychic level. Likewise, anything violating the *ḥr* principles will cause disintegration both in the universal and at the individual levels.

The universal and individual dimensions of *ḥr* (human rights) regulate human behaviour. The social connotations of *ḥr* laws are very large. *Ḥr* laws are the expressions of the divine law-giver so that people may live according to the rhythms of reality. The mystics say: "by following *ṛta*, man becomes established in *satya* achieving a fuller and more harmonious existence". The United Nations say that *by following the ḥr laws man becomes established in peace and harmony.* Police, as a law enforcement agency can establish harmonious existence only if they render their services in a human rights friendly way—according to *dharma* and *ṛta.*

The mystical insight that the norm of human behaviour must correspond to the *ṛta* —the natural rhythm of the universe—has decisively influenced, directly and indirectly the human rights consciousness of the world community. In Indian mysticism, it is taught that the Supreme Spirit—Prajapati—orders the Nature's Rhythm and in the world today, the international consensus (which may be identified as the Supreme Spirit of the mysticism) influences the rhythm of the universe. Indian mystics brought the concept of *dharma* to enforce the *ṛta* and the world community brought international consensus to enforce the *ṛta.* In formulating the *dharma* in a specific way, the mystical seers spoke about the norms of behaviour for each social class, each stage of life etc. Likewise, in formulating the world consensus for enforcing human rights law, the United Nations spoke about human rights of people in various areas such as law enforcement, labour, punishment, delinquency etc. And in both—*i.e.,* in *dharma* and in U.N. Declarations—the norms of behaviour were formulated basing on the universal moral principles.

Indian mysticism classifies *dharma* into two categories—and they are (1) *Sadharanadharma* and (2) *Svadharma.* The former is intended to help a person to lead a life worthy of a man and it means nothing but a life of a human rights friendly way. The mystical seers insist that everyone must follow these general rules of conduct and they are—

1. *ahimsa* (non-injury)
2. *ksama* (forbearance)
3. *indriyanigraha* (self-control)
4. *daya* (compassion)
5. *dana* (charity)
6. *sauca* (purity)
7. *satya* (truth)
8. *tapas* (penance)

9. *jnana* (wisdom).

A close scrutiny of all the U.N. Declarations and Conventions may reveal that the entire human rights laws are just the reproductions of the *Sadharanadharma* taught by the mystical seers.

For example—

1. "Corporal punishment, punishment by placing in a dark cell, and all cruel, inhuman or degrading punishment shall be completely prohibited as punishments for disciplinary offences" (Rule 31 of the Standard Minimum Rules for the Treatment of Prisoners, Resolution adopted by the United Nations on 30, August, 1955). This is nothing but the rule of *ahimsa* (non-injury) of *Sadharanadharma.*
2. "Whenever the lawful use of force and firearms is unavoidable, law enforcement officials shall: (a) exercise restraint in such use and act in proportion to the seriousness of the offence and the legitimate objectives to be achieved" [Principle 5(a) of the Basic Principles on the Use of Force and Firearms by Law Enforcement officials]. This is the *dharma-principle* called *ksama* (forbearance).
3. (i) "It shall be prohibited to take undue advantage of the situation of a detained or imprisoned person for the purpose of compelling him to confess, to incriminate himself otherwise or to testify against any other person. (ii) No detained person while being interrogated shall be subject of interrogation which impair his capacity of decision or his judgement" [Principle 21 (1 and 2) of the Body of Principles for the Protection of All Persons under Any Form of Detention or Imprisonment]. This is the principle of *Indriyanigraha* (self-control) of *Sadharanadharma.*
4. "Persons below 18 years of age at the time of the commission of the crime shall not be sentenced to death,

nor shall the death sentence be carried out on pregnant women, or on new mothers, or on persons who have become insane" (cf. Safeguards guaranteeing protection of the rights of those facing the death penalty) and it expresses the rule of *daya* (compassion) taught by *Sadharana-dharma.* Likewise we may see that almost all human rights proclaimed by the United Nations are just the replica or reproduction of the inspired truths by the mystical seers.

Manu gives nine rules and they are the human rights laws. They are—

1. forbearance, 2. forgiveness, 3. control over mind and heart, 4. non-stealing, 5. Purity, 6. control over senses and intellect, 7. knowledge, 8. truth and 9. freedom from anger. Any number of examples from the U.N. Declarations/Conventions can be brought to show that they contain only those things which were revealed by the Indian sages from ancient times—long before the westerners had thought about human rights!

For example—

"Everyone is entitled to all the rights and freedoms" (Article 2, U.D.H.R.) and it being the truth, the U.N. cannot but proclaim it to the world community. The *Arthasastra* of Kautilya too lists the principles of human conduct and they are today called the human rights laws by the international community. *Mahabharata*, in a nutshell, puts down everything which the United Nations have spoken so far on human rights under their various Declarations and Conventions.

"What is harmful to oneself, one should not do to others. This is the quintessence of *dharma*" (*Mahabharata,* XIII, cxviii, 8).

If the world community accepts this principle set forth by *Mahabharata*, then all the U.N. Declarations/Conventions cease to have any meaning or relevance today. But, the people fail to or refuse to follow the mystical laws and principles! The nations of the world close their eyes to the eternal truths revealed by the Indian mystics. The rich nations ignore human rights principles. It being the reality, the United Nations speak in loud voice to inspire and instigate the world community to follow the revealed truths that the human rights should be recognized and human dignity must be respected.

Svadharma means the specific responsibilities incumbent on individuals in accordance to his stage of life and his social position. A police officer has a social position and he has authority and power. He can misuse his authority and abuse his power and the United Nations have taken note of this hard reality. They have enacted (1) Convention Against Torture and Other Cruel, Inhuman or Degrading Treatment or Punishment; (2) Protection of the Human Rights of Victims of Crime and Abuse of Power; (3) Body of Principles for the Protection of All Persons under Any Form of Detention or Imprisonment etc. There are many more. In all such Declarations, the world community sees only *svadharma* which is based on the *sadharanadharma* being applied to individuals depending upon their position, character and abilities. In *Gita*, Krishna tells:

"It is better to perform one's own obligations poorly than to do another's well" (*Gita*, 3, 45; 18. 47). In the Code of Conduct for Law Enforcement Officers, in the Basic Principles for the Treatment of Prisoners, in the United Nations' Standard Minimum Rules for the Administration of juvenile justice and in many other Declarations/Conventions, the United Nations just bring out the *Svadharma* of individuals.

Indian mystical truths are truths of eternal values and they tell about the goals of human life. Human rights laws too are laws of eternal values and they also speak about the goals of human life. Human rights ensure the ordered course of life in harmony with people's desire to establish world peace by respecting human rights just like the *dharma* ensures happiness in tune with the *ṛta* of the universe. The innermost self of man (*atman*) is identical with the ultimate ground of the universe (*Brahman*) and this truth is the basis of human rights, human dignity and human existence.

"Who so thus knows 'I am Brahman' becomes this all". Again: Who so knows *Brahman* wins the all highest" (*Taittiriya Upanishad*, 2, 1; *Brihadaranyaka Upanishad*, 1, 4, 10).

12

Hinduism, Hindu Mysticism, Human Rights and United Nations

What is Hinduism? According to Dr. S. Radhakrishnan, "the term 'Hindu' had originally a territorial and not a credal significance. It implied residence in a well defined geographical area. Aboriginal tribes, savage and half-civilized people, the cultured Dravidians and the Vedic Aryans were all Hindus as they were the sons of the same mother. The Hindu thinkers reckoned with the striking fact that the men and women dwelling in India belonged to different communities, worshipped different gods, and practised different rites". Whatever that be, Hinduism in its deeper analysis is a religion—a kind of life or experience. It is *darsana—i.e.,* an insight into the nature of reality and an *anubhava—i.e.,* an experience of reality. As there exist the *darsana* and *anubhava,* necessarily, human rights and respect for human person come there. Mahatma Gandhi says: "If I were asked to define the Hindu creed, I should simply say: "search after truth through non-violent means. A man may or may not believe in God and still call himself a Hindu. Hinduism is a relentless pursuit after truth.....Hinduism is the religion of truth. Truth is God. Denial of God we have known. Denial of truth we have not known."

What is this 'search after truth through non-violent means?' It is for this search after truth the United Nations stand for—the world community desires for and they have expressed their wish in the Charter of the United Nations "to reaffirm faith in fundamental human rights, in the dignity and worth of human person, in the equal rights of men and women and of nations, large or small" and for this purpose "to practice tolerance and live together in peace with one another as good neighbours" and "to employ international machinery for the promotion of the economic and social advancement of all peoples". Hinduism stood for "human rights, human dignity, human worth, equal rights for man and woman, tolerance, living together and what not?" Dr. S. Radhakrishnan again says: "Hindu religion can be described in one word, that is, "do the right". Jawaharlal Nehru, in his *Discovery of India* says that Hinduism in "its essential spirit seems to be to live and let live" and what do the United Nations speak about human rights? Their essential spirit seems to be 'to live and let live'. Hinduism has a philosophy in its background. It has a religion in its background and they are traceable to the *Vedas, Upanishads,* the *Agamas* and the *Bhagavad Gita* and they cannot be wrong, for, the Hindu philosophy and theology survived many centuries" and in the words of J.R. Goyal: "India has been great because she has been the cradle of Hinduism".

The *Vedas* bring together all human rights in one way or other. The mystical seers had the intuition of human rights violations and, therefore, they brought principles for guiding the people and the United Nations just took them, knowingly or unknowingly, for guiding the people by Declarations and Conventions.

"The wise know that truth and untruth are always competing against each other" (*Ṛg Veda* 7, 104, 12) and this is what is seen in the fight between the acceptance and negation of human rights in the world. There are many people and nations in the world and they are incapable of having insight into human realities. They violate human rights and the mystical truths and inspired revelations make the people understand the reality. They are to guide the people to truths and the United Nations, in fact, do the same thing with the support of the world community. Hindus believe that God reveals many things through men and the mystical seers were those who had the privilege of having the divine experience, revelations, inspiration and intuition. Hindus believe further that God continues his revelation and it may be through sages, seers or through saints. The United Nations may be a means by which God reveals His wisdom and love.

"If the whole race of man, in every land, of every colour, and every stage of culture, is the offspring of God, then we must admit that, in the vast compass of His providence, all are being trained by His wisdom and supported by His love to reach within the limits of their powers a knowledge of the Supreme" (Dr. S. Radhakrishnan). He continues:

"When the Hindu found that different people aimed at and achieved God-realization in different ways, they generously recognized them all and justified their place in the course of history". The United Nations too found:

"Whereas recognition of the inherent dignity and of the equal and inalienable rights of all members of the human family is the foundation of freedom, justice and peace in the world" (see, U.D.H.R., Preamble) and just like the Hindu who recognized human truths, the world community too recognized them through a Declaration and it was called the Universal Declaration of Human Rights.

Universal Declaration of Human Rights and Hinduism

The *Atman* is *Bhahman* and the *Brahman* is *Atman.* In the *Upanishads*, one reads *"Tat tvam asi* (That thou art) and *Aham Brahmasmi* (I am *Brahman*). What more does one want to say that the *human person* must be recognized everywhere? In Article 1, U.D.H.R., it is affirmed that *all human beings are born in equal dignity and rights*—Humanism is the dominant note in the Universal Declaration of Human Rights. Humanness is expressed in service to humanity, universal brotherhood, humanism, respect for human dignity, person and freedom. Indian mysticism says that humanity as a whole is bound in unity, "People are endowed with reason and conscience and should act towards one another in a spirit of brotherhood" (U.D.H.R.).

Indian mystical seers and visionaries may not be human rights activists, but their intuitions and inspirations are more than human rights activism as they are the true sources of human rights movement everywhere. The inspired truths descend from the highest perceptions of the soul. The narrowness of people down the centuries compels them to involve in human rights violations. Human rights violations are evils and for the mystics, any evil is an imperfection of the world.

"Give up all evils even here" (*Atharva Veda* 12, 2, 27). This is the mystical revelation. "A man of evil thoughts engenders hatred which brings misery" (*Uttradhain Sutra,* 32, 18). The United Nations just brought out this sublime truth when they said:

"Whereas disregard and contempt for human rights have resulted in barbarous acts which have outraged the conscience of mankind......". (U.D.H.R. Preamble). What to do? Human rights must be respected—stated the United Nations; evils must be avoided—stated the mystical seers.

"As a rich merchant without companion should abandon a dangerous road, or as a man who wishes to live should get rid of poison, so one should give up all evil". (*Dhammapada,* 9, 8). There is no other way to get out of the danger.

"Whereas it is essential if man is not to be compelled to have recourse, as a last resort, to rebellion against tyranny and oppression, that human rights should be protected by law" (United Nations U.D.H.R. Preamble). There is no other way to get out of the danger. Besides the *Vedas, Upanishads* etc. the truths are revealed in all Hindu *scriptures*—the *Mahabharata,* the *Gita* etc. The scriptures instruct that all people must honour the inspired truths.

"He who, ignoring the teachings of Scriptures, acts according to his will, cannot attain success, nor happiness nor emancipation. Therefore, to determine what ought to be done and what ought not to be done, scripture is the authority" (*Gita,* 18, 23, 24). If this is what the seers say, the United Nations insist that all people and nations must abide by what is proclaimed by the United Nations with the consensus of the world community.

In the exercise of his rights and freedoms, everyone shall be subject only to such limitations as are determined by law solely for the purpose of securing due recognition and respect for the rights and freedoms of others and of meeting the just requirements of morality, public order and the general welfare in democratic society.

"These rights and freedoms may in no case be exercised contrary to the purposes and principles of the United Nations". (U.D.H.R., Article 29). And in essence, what the Indian scriptures say and what the United Nations say are one and the same thing as far as human rights and respect to human person are concerned. For every man is created by God. There is a human content in everything.

Lila, Maya, Karma and Human Rights

In Indian mysticism, the *Brahman* is the ultimate reality and as said earlier, the *Atman* is *Brahman* and the *Brahman* is *Atman.* The *Brahman* is infinite, eternal, immortal and Atman is not a part of the Absolute. For, the *Brahman* cannot be divided and limited to manyness. There is no individual *Atman* or soul in the real sense. The *Brahman* alone is real. What more one needs to say about man?—his sublimity?—his worth?—his greatness? Human rights must be respected.

There is the reference in the *Upanishads* about two *souls* in man—*i.e.,* the *lower* and the *real.* The *lower* is the *ego* which takes part in the universe and the *higher* is the *Atman.* The *Atman* is not limited in time and space. It is Absolute, *Brahman,* Truth, Bliss and Consciousness. What more one wants to affirm the loftiness of man? There is only one *Atman* in an individual and it is the infinite *Being.* As the *Atman* is infinite, it cannot be more than one. The infinite *Atman* can be only one and precisely, there cannot be many souls on earth. But there are many people and they are the unreal reflections of the *Brahman.* The *Atman* is reflected on different centres of *Maya* and gives birth to many finite souls on earth. But the real *Atman* is not the reflected image.

People perceive the world to be real, but actually it is not so. As the Absolute alone is real and it is transcendental. It is unmanifest, but the world is manifest. The world is perceptible to us, but it does not exist. *Maya* explains this contradiction inherent in the world. *Maya* says that the world is real from the empirical point of view. From the transcendental point of view, the world is unreal. From the spiritual and transcendental point of view, the world is pure illusion. Man sees the world by the help of his five senses. *Maya* says that one must see the world through another sense in which case, it will appear as something different. For, the world has no real existence. Everything in the world—matter, mind, self etc.—are ultimately unreal. They are real only in the empirical sense. People are born in *Maya.* They live in *Maya* and die in it. The world and everything in it exist in the Absolute and they exist in the Absolute as the snake (an illusion) exists in the rope. As a result, people perceive the rope as snake. The rope does not change into snake. Similarly, the Absolute does not change into anything in the world. Everything in the world is the appearance of the Absolute. Hence, *Brahman* only exists in the real sense and people see the manifoldness. As long as man is in ignorance, he sees the world as real. When he is free from his ignorance, he perceives the Absolute alone in everything.

Why there is human right violation in the world? It is because the people are in ignorance. They are in *Maya* and they cannot see the Absolute, *Brahman,* in everyone. So long as a man is in ignorance, he commits human rights violation. He fails to see *Brahman* in every individual.

"Everyone is entitled to all the rights and freedoms set forth in this Declaration, without distinction of any kind, such as race, colour, sex, language, religion, political or other opinion, national or social origin, property, birth or other status.

Furthermore, no distinction shall be made on the basis of the political, jurisdictional or international status of the country or territory to which a person belongs whether it be independent, trust, non-self-governing or under any other limitations of sovereignty" (U.D.H.R., Article 2). This Article of the United Nations may be the desire of the world community to have a change in people who must be behaving from their ignorance. They must not be in *Maya* and must see the Absolute in every one without distinction of any kind such as race, sex, colour, language, religion etc. Whenever a man fails to see the Absolute in another, he sees only the *rope* and he perceives the *rope as the snake.* Every man on earth is really the appearance of God.

> "When one is in ignorance, he sees the phenomena and does not see God. When he sees God, this universe vanishes entirely for Him" (Vivekananda).

Why do people commit human rights violations? *Maya* explains this. Take for example the fact that the policeman tortures a suspect to obtain a confession from him. They do so because they have dominance over the suspects in their custody. The police have dominance over the suspects and they do not have dominance over the law and law courts. Suppose that the suspect is interrogated in front of a court of law, then the police do not have dominance over the suspect. Then they respect the law and the laws governing police interrogation. In such a situation there will not be human rights violations. The contradiction of human rights violations and human rights friendly approaches remains a true fact only in the police stations and not in the courts of law. One may see such contradictions in this world and it is because there exists *"Maya"* in this world.

Policemen have to be informed of the influence of *Maya* and for it, the United Nations proclaim—

> "Everyone has the right to life, liberty and security of person" (U.D.H.R., Article 3).

> "No one shall be subjected to torture or to cruel, inhuman or degrading treatment or punishment" (U.D.H.R., Article 5).

The policemen must see the *Absolute* in everyone including the suspects, the arrestees, the detinues and so on. Whenever a man in police custody feels that he is unjustly treated—in a human rights unfriendly way—then, he is. Only a human right friendly treatment can give him justice and happiness. When a policeman, as anybody else, is possessed of wisdom, the illusion that he is more than what he really is gets vanished. Then, he perceives the Absolute in the suspect, in the arrestee, in the detinue and in everybody. The world of justice administration is an illusion for an ignorant policeman. For him, it is a mirage. He must realize that the power and authority given to him by law is for human welfare and justice administration. Everything done in a human rights unfriendly way does not take anybody to anywhere except to miscarriage of justice. He sees a mirage of lake in a desert and if he does so, he suffers from illusion. On a closer observation, he will understand that the lake is merely sand and sand alone and nothing else. When he comes to such a realization, he is no longer deceived. To a knower of human dignity, all illusions disappear and he perceives *Brahman*, the unchangeable, vast and infinite consciousness in all people. This is otherwise called human rights friendly policing and this is what the United Nations insist:

> "All are equal before the law and are entitled without any discrimination to equal protection of the law. All are entitled to equal protection against any discrimination in violation of this Declaration and against any incitement to such discrimination" (U.D.H.R., Article 7).
> "Everyone has the right to recognition everywhere as a person before law" (U.D.H.R., Article 6).

How can the police arrest a person arbitrarily if they are free from ignorance—from *Maya*? They cannot and whenever they do so, they fail to see the *Brahman* in others.

> "No one shall be subjected to arbitrary arrest, detention or exile" (U.D.H.R., Article 9).

Lila and Cosmic Evolution

Hinduism teaches that the creation of the world is through the self-sacrifice of God. Here the God becomes the world which, in the end, becomes again God. The creative activity of the God is called *Lila—i.e.,* the play of God. According to Sri Aurobindo, one of the greatest mystics of the modern world, creation and manifestations are the two Divine Processes. Creation for Aurobindo means the descent of the Divine into matter or lower forms of realities. He brings the concept of *cosmic evolution.* He feels that human evolution is a fact and it is towards a higher and spiritual consciousness and power. Respect for human rights, it is felt by many, is an evolution towards higher and better world order. The world moves towards a new world order wherein human rights are respected.

"Everyone has the right to freedom of thought, conscience and religion" (U.D.H.R., Article 18).

"Everyone has the right to freedom of opinion and expression" (U.D.H.R., Article 19).

Everyone has the right to freedom of peaceful assembly and association" (U.D.H.R., Article 20).

"Everyone has the right to take part in the government of his country" (U.D.H.R., Article 21).

"Everyone has the right to equal access to public service in his country" (U.D.H.R., Article 21).

"Everyone has the right to social security" (U.D.H.R., Article 22).

"Everyone has the right to work" and "everyone, without any discrimination, has the right to equal pay for equal work" (U.D.H.R., Article 23).

Thus one sees a new world order. Sri Aurobindo says that the destiny of a man is not to remain man for ever, but to be a divine being with omniscience, omnipotence and bliss. Likewise, the people think that the attempt of the United Nations is to create a new world order by transforming people from their human right unfriendly approaches to human rights friendly approaches. The destiny of the world, the international community thinks, is not to remain in human rights unfriendly way for ever, but to be human rights friendly. The world community, I believe, is destined to be transformed into a human rights friendly community and finally to create a new world wherein human rights are respected. The mystical teachings and inspired truths open the eyes of people to realities of life. The U.N. Declarations and Conventions further proclaim these mystical teachings and revealed truths from international platforms so that a world-consensus is created. When the international consensus is reached for a transformation, necessarily it works and the ignorance, *Maya,* removed. When we analyse the mystic teachings of the seers from *Ṛg Veda* up to now, we find that everyone wants to establish a new world order wherein human rights are respected and recognized. Some nations of the world—or some people—may refuse to recognize human rights. They are in ignorance—in *Maya*—and there is the need to wipe off their ignorance. The whole world is rushing for acceptance of human rights and if any country is not accepting human rights, then it means that such country does so only temporarily. They will—will have to—accept human rights in due course. The evolution towards acceptance of human rights is a fact and it is certainly for the creation of a new world order wherein the man is respected and recognized as *Brahman* in Indian mysticism. When the world community will have the illumination, light, brightness, thoughts, consciousness etc., then a new world order comes into being.

Karma and Human Rights

In the Hindu view of nature, *Karma* means '*action*' or '*deed*'. Hinduism believes that any action brings some effects on the organism and on the environment. Any human rights friendly approach brings corresponding effects and necessarily a new world order, harmony and peace. Any human rights unfriendly approach brings chaos and rebellion against it. Police behaviour which is human rights friendly brings fame, name, acceptance and recognition for police service. What do the police achieve by their human rights unfriendly attitudes and approaches? Nothing, rather, blame, reproach and non-recognition of their services to humanity.

"No one shall be subjected to arbitrary interference with his privacy, family, home or correspondence, nor to attacks upon his honour and reputation. Everyone has the right to the protection of the law against such interference or attacks" (U.D.H.R., Article 12). If the police violate this law in human rights, the police invariably bring ill-name to themselves. Such behaviours show lack of self-esteem and human respect, lack of culture and respect for *Brahman* in a person.

Indian mysticism holds the view that each single word, thought or deed enters into the organism of the self and *karma* forms the character, reputation, worthiness of the self and individual. Good *karma* produces good effects and bad *karma* produces bad effects.

Police are what they are because of their past doings—*karma* and if they have a good name, it means that they did good *karma*. Police organisation has a history and a future. If they want to make a bright future for them, then they have to be human rights friendly by doing good *karma.* Police *karma* has two aspects—retrospective and prospective. If the police actions today is based on the character and inherited behaviour patterns of the past, they do not become free actions. They may be human rights unfriendly and that is the reason why police are told to behave in a human rights friendly way.

"Everyone is entitled in full equality, to a fair and public hearing by an independent and impartial tribunal, in the determination of his rights and obligations and of any criminal charge against him" (U.D.H.R., Article 10). But some policemen may say that a suspect is likely to get an acquittal from the court after a trial and, therefore, he must be handled in a police way (meaning human rights unfriendly way) before his trial. This behaviour pattern may have a past and whenever the policeman sticks to the past ill-doings, he simply refuses to exercise his freedom to be human rights friendly.

Every human action is motivated and a police action is not an exemption to this general rule. The purpose of police actions in the new world order, doubtlessly, is human rights friendly in nature. Precisely, therefore, the police must learn lessons from their past and utilise them to their future. The past *karmas* of police can be made beneficial for making the police human rights friendly—to make some good out of them.

Police job can be compared to a game of cards. The play should not be a gambling—*i.e.*, a game of chance, but must be a game of skill. A good player utilizes his cards skilfully in the best manner by studying the various options and alternatives and finding out the best out of them. A bad player may not do so. The policeman has to play the game observing all the rules of the game. If he does not, he will be sent out as a misfit—a man who is ignorant. Likewise, a policeman who wants to enforce the laws, then he must enforce them by observing the laws and not at all by violating the laws. Anybody who violates laws to enforce laws does a great disservice to man and humanity.

Karma and rebirth go together in Hinduism. Police has a past and certainly, today's police come from the past and doubtlessly they are developing into a future—into a world of new order. A rebirth is expected. The police is imperfect today and it moves on perpetually for fulfilment and perfection. And the perfection, figuratively, means a human rights friendly police service—a rebirth of a police system which has a continuity with the past (*karma*) and a creative advance into the future (freedom). The bad deeds which the police did in the past could be transformed to good deeds through their *karma* in the future. As *karma* has its effects i.e., a rebirth depending upon the *Karma* is inevitable. The fact of rebirth has been acknowledged by many in the East and in the West. Pythagoras, Plato, Empedocles, Plotinus, Hume, Schopenhauer, *Vedas* and all systems of Indian philosophy accepted rebirth. The United Nations want a rebirth by accepting human rights of people and that is what they mean by a *new world order*.

Fritjof Capra in his "*The Tao of Physics*" writes:

"To be free from the spell of *Maya*, to break the bonds of *karma* means to realize that all the phenomena we perceive with our senses are part of the same reality. It means to experience, conceitely and personally, that everything including our own self, is *Brahman*. This experience is called *moksha* or liberation in Hindu philosophy and it is the very essence of Hinduism".

Moksha

Hindu mystics think that the man is composed of soul and body. The body is perishable and the soul is not. It is immortal and eternal. It is *Brahman* itself. *Moksha* or liberation means the realization of the *soul's* identity with the *Brahman*. Swami Vivekananda speaks of *Jivan Mukthi and Videha Mukthi*. *Jivan Mukthi* is a state of freedom realized in one's own life-time. In *Videha Mukthi*, the self reposes in eternal identity with *Brahman* whereas in *Jivan Mukthi*, the self remains tied with the body. It is due to the binding effects of the acquired *karma*. In *Videha Mukthi*, the liberated soul becomes one with the Absolute which is truth, existence, consciousness and bliss. The *Atman* and *Brahman* are one. In such a situation, there is no ignorance, no pain, no sufferings, no ego, no rebirth and the soul realizes eternal freedom, everlasting bliss and infinite existence. This is the greatness of man and there is no distinction here. This is the basis of human rights which repeatedly insist that all human beings are equal in dignity and rights.

Advaita Vedanta says that *Moksha* is a state of absorption of the selves into the Absolute—the *Brahman* and consequent dissolution of the body, life and mind. But, there are other interpretations as well for *Moksha*. Tagore, for example, rejects the *Advaida* view and holds the view that there is no other universe where the self unites with *Brahman*. The self unites with the Absolute on this earth. He writes:

"Deliverance? Where is this deliverance to be found? Our master himself has joyfully taken upon himself the bonds of creation, he is bound with us all for ever". Accordingly, God himself created the world and He is bound in love with men. This is the sublimity of human birth and the foundation of human rights. The United Nations say in the Preamble of the Universal Declaration of Human Rights that "whereas recognition of the inherent dignity and of the equal and inalienable rights of all members of the human family is the foundation of freedom, justice and peace in the world" and the mystics may say that the foundation of human rights lies in the fact that everyman/woman is the creation of God. There is a universality of mystical experience and the mystics of the world whether Hindu, Christian or Muslim say the samething in different languages at different times. "One cannot honestly", observes Underhill, "that there is any wide difference between the *Brahmin*, the Sufi or the Christian mystics at their best".

Jnanayoga and Human Rights

'*Yoga*' means 'to yoke', 'to join' etc. and it has two meanings in Indian philosophy. Firstly, it means the union of an individual self to the Absolute. The second meaning of *yoga* is path, method, means or discipline by the help and practice of which one may realize salvation. A *jnanayogi* admits that all people, irrespective of their caste, creed, sex, education, status, race, etc., are the manifestations of one indeterminate, nameless, formless, eternal and infinite reality of *Brahman*. A true seeker of truth practices tolerance and universal acceptance of everybody. Why there are human rights violations? *Jnanayoga* may explain the reasons as:

1. People are reluctant to renounce the worldly desires and possessions. They want to have more worldly fortunes. A corrupt police officer, for instance, is human rights unfriendly in his attitude and approaches.
2. Failure/reluctance to control one's senses and passions. For example, torturing the suspects under custody.
3. Failure/refusal to have a rational understanding that *Brahman* alone is real. Everyman/woman is *Brahman*.
4. Lack of any sincere desire for *Moksha*/liberation.

In fact human rights unfriendly people/nations do not want liberation from the evils of human rights violations. Even after 50 years of the existence of the Universal Declaration of Human Rights, there are people/nations which do not accept human rights whole-heartedly or if at all they accept human rights, they do so with difficulty and reluctance.

Some people may subscribe to the view that every police

officer/man must be a *karmayogi,* meaning thereby that he must exercise his power and authority with detachment. A king may live in a palace, but may remain quite unaffected and calm. On the other hand, a poor man living in a hut may be deeply attached with the pleasures of the world. Likewise, a policeman can perform his work without violating the human rights of people. Police service consists in rendering selfless work. One must not do police job for selfishness. Whenever selfishness comes, there is the chance of becoming human rights unfriendly. The effect of performing human rights friendly policing is one's own self purification. By doing so, the policemen realize eternal bliss.

There are two types of actions and they are called *Pravritti* and *Nivritti.* Acts which constantly bind a man come under *Pravritti.* The pursuit for wealth, power, authority, name, fame, etc. comes under *Pravritti* which in turn leads to bondage. In such instances, the acts will be human rights unfriendly. If the work is done with detachment from the empirical self, then it becomes moral and to that extent, human rights friendly. Acts which are done by police in renunciation for administering just justice, then such acts are called *Nivritti.*

"It is the theory of non-attachment, to be attached to nothing while doing our work of life. Know that you are separated entirely from the world, but that you are in the world and that whenever you may be doing in it, you are not doing that for your own self." (*Gita*).

Gita teaches: "Do not give up the world, imbibe its influences as much as you can, but if it be for your own enjoyment's sake, work not at all". This is *karmayoga* and that is what the police must do for the people. For it, the police must control their self and must remain detached to the result of their actions. Any police officer/man who utters epithets, employs torture, exerts coercion on suspects is not a *karmayogi* rather is a human rights violator. A police officer/man has to fight evils ceaselessly and it also includes fighting evils within himself. Swami Vivekananda teaches:

"Resist all evils, mental and physical and when you have

succeeded in resisting, then will calmness come." The United Nations too desire peace, harmony and calmness in the world and they think that respect shown to the human rights of people can only ensure calmness among people and nations. Everyone, in that sense, must be a *karmayogi* who must do good works, ethical and moral, showing respect to others and with self-esteem and human dignity. Universal love is a theme taught by *bhaktiyoga.* A lover of God sees everything belonging to God. He perceives the mankind as God. "*Bhaktiyoga* is the path of systematised devotion for the attainment of union with the Absolute"—says Swami Vivekananda. Anybody in *bhaktiyoga* will be necessarily a human rights friendly person.

Hinduism tells about *Raja-yoga* which is a method for realization of salvation through the control of one's mind. *Raja-yoga* puts down eight disciplines—*Yama, Niyama, Asana, Pranayama, Pratyahara, Dharana, Dhyana* and *Samadhi*—for self realization. *Raja-yoga* speaks about the purity of conduct. *Yama,* for example, consists of (1) non-injury, truthfulness, non-covetousness, chastity and not accepting anything from another. A lover of human rights must have purity of conduct. For example, anybody who accepts gifts from other is impure and to that extent is human rights unfriendly. Corruption, illegal gratification, graft, political influence in police functioning—all these make the service impure and human rights unfriendly. *Niyama,* for instance again, consists in the cultivation of good habits. *Raja-yoga* helps for internal purification of mind and it consists in acquiring love, brotherhood, kindness and human consideration. In fact, the Declarations and Conventions of the United Nations are above love, brotherhood, kindness and human consideration.

When one reads *Bhagavad Gita,* he learns how Lord Krishna teaches human rights. Lord Krishna leads people to righteous actions. Righteous pursuit of duties forms, *inter alia,* a theme of *Gita* and the U.N. Declarations and Conventions contain many of the inspired truths taught by Lord Krishna. The war in *Gita* is fought for the removal of social evils just like the world community fights against human rights violations which are social evils/ills. People want a new world order where human rights are recognized and respected and the war in *Bhagavad Gita* was fought for the sake of restoration of an ethical or moral universe. The war in *Gita* was for the creation of a new social order—for the removal of a tyrannous king. Here too, the war by the international community is for eradicating evil practices violating human rights. For fighting against social evils, God descended from heaven to earth and that is what one sees in *Gita*. Here, the world community comes forward for fighting against human rights violations—social evils in every sense of the word. .

Hindu Mysticism and Human Rights

Mysticism etiologically comes from Greek *mysters* which means 'one who is initiated' (New Age Encyclopaedia). A mystic is a person who is blessed with a capacity to have communion or union with the supernatural. The mystics are called *seers* and transcend earthly experience and they feel a oneness with extra-earthly. Human rights as they are known today may not have been heard by the mystics, nevertheless, as *seers*, they have *Darshana* which reveals to them human rights principles as well. They become one with the supernatural and reveal inspired truths. They have spiritual ecstasy. Mysticism is a striking feature of Hinduism. The *Vedas* and *Upanishads* contain many mystical revelations and many of them teach the unity of the individual soul (*Atman*) and the Absolute, the cosmic soul (*Brahman*). This unity of *Atman* and *Brahman* makes every human person respectable and reveals the human dignity. This is the basis of human rights. One sees fraternity, equality, selflessness, dignity, wisdom, freedom, courage, sacrifice, tolerance, decency, discipline of senses and passion, truthfulness, love, consideration, sympathy and many more human qualities—human rights friendly qualities—in Indian mystical revelations, for, the mystical seers are humanists. They speak about socialization of humanity and it is nothing but recognition of human rights. The mystical seers have intuition which reveals the truths of many things. Human rights violations are realities in the world and precisely, therefore, the seers want to eradicate such social evils.

United Nations bring out the principles in human rights after collecting data based on sense-experience. They conduct discussions, seminars, workshops, consultations, conferences and thus arrive at consensus after analysing the sense-data on human rights violations. They frame general laws. The mystics arrive at conclusions on the basis cf intuition and thus the *ṛsis* talk about eternal truths. The revealed truths through intuitive knowledge give an insight into the whole reality. Hence, the intuitive knowledge will be fully true, eternal and infinite. In ecstasy, the seers experience the totality of consciousness. As such, the mystical knowledge is spontaneous or immediate. It comes to the mystic as a vision. Hence, intuition has the character of revelation. The mystics are the chosen people of God. They see realities and speak them out. What the United Nations spoke in 1948 about human rights, the mystical sages could see long back—several centuries ago. The intuition comes to a seer as a flash—as a revelation. The mystics experience infinite consciousness, power and blessedness. Hinduism says that the intuitive consciousness of the seer is identical with *Brahman*. Hinduism thinks further: "to know the Supreme *Brahman* is to become that *Brahman*".

The mystical revelation is that a change is possible through a change in the *selves* and it is 100 per cent true in the case of recognition and acceptance of human rights. United Nations think of enforcing human rights through legal enactments. Enforcement of human rights is different from embracing human rights. The former is through an outward force and the latter is through a transformation of human attitudes to others. Hindus believe that human rights must be practised through *karmayoga*. To be human rights friendly is to be bound to God. When God governs man's thoughts, ideals, emotions, activities, sentiments, attitudes and behaviour, he becomes human rights friendly. United Nations think that their Declarations and Conventions can make people human rights friendly. Each may bring effects in its own way.

Human rights, as the United Nations think, are the rights of people towards their life, liberty, dignity and equality. Indian mysticism speak more than what the United Nations say in this area. Humanism, equality, brotherhood, peace, harmony, freedom, self-realization, salvation, cosmic evolution, spiritualization, divinisation and many more areas are revealed to the mystics. In that way, the mystical revelations are more comprehensive than what has been proclaimed by the United Nations. The United Nations have, on close scrutiny, codified the mystical revelations in their Declarations and Conventions. The world is more compact today. Humanity has come closer and closer today. The people have an international forum to think together, speak together and act together. The values, culture, tradition of many countries influence one another. The values become universal and they do not recognize any borders. The United Nations accept the challenges and they unite the east and the west, the north and the south and come to a consensus that the human rights must be respected. They proclaim to the world the mystical perceptions and experiences of the sages. The *Vedas, Upanishads, Puranas, Bhagavad Gita,* Buddha, Jain scriptures, Christianity, Islam, Taoism, Plato, and the values taught by them influence the thinking of the United Nations. The mystical experiences of the *ṛsis* and sages serve as data for the world community to arrive at a consensus on human rights. No doubt, the United Nations cannot bring out the Declarations and Conventions just by accumulation of sense-data. They, knowingly or unknowingly, base their principles on the deep intuitive and mystical truths revealed by the saints. For, the mystics have intuitive encounters with the Divine, the Absolute. The mystical experiences of the seers belonging to all religions in the world may be the same as they come from the same source and what we see today is that the United Nations have just organized them in a system—in their Declarations and Conventions. The United Nations arrive at eternal truths from many sources and one of the most important sources is the mystical experiences of the seers from time antiquity.

13

Human Rights: Eastern and Western

Human rights are for human beings and there cannot be any distinction in human rights for the eastern and western people. Human rights recognize no borders and all rights are for all under the sun and on earth. Nevertheless, a question is asked—may be out of curiosity, and the question is: "Do the people all over the world enjoy human rights alike?"—in other words, "can the people everywhere enjoy human rights alike?" No, the answer is an emphatic no. Why? Take for example—the police and human rights. Human rights law says that torture by police is a human right violation, O.K., it is so. At the same time, the police have to find out the truth when they investigate crimes—or when they interrogate suspects. How should the police interrogate suspects? The answer is simple and that is: "interrogate a suspect in a scientific and psychological way". What are the scientific and psychological ways? There is no answer to the question. Are the police taught about the scientific and psychological ways? Police in well advanced countries or in developed nations may give an answer which is different from what is given by the police in a developing country and their answer may be different in an undeveloped country. The objective of police investigation in all countries may be the same, but the ways of achieving the objective may be different in different countries. They vary very much depending upon how well the police are trained in scientific and psychological interrogation/investigation. The infrastructural facilities in developed countries for the police may be very fine, but the same for the police in developing/underdeveloped countries, may be far away from being satisfactory. One cannot insist all policemen everywhere in the world to behave in a particular way. The western approach seems to be to enforce human rights vigorously by enacting laws, rules and legislations. It does not look into the ground realities. The human rights activists in the west think that the ground level situations in all countries are exactly as they are in their country. This view is simply not correct. Human rights consciousness can never be imposed by an external force by punishment or by giving compensation in cash etc. The consciousness must come from within and that is what is seen in eastern approaches. The mystic seers and the sacred scriptures in India made attempts to inculcate human rights values into the souls of the people whereas the western approach was to enforce the same through aggressive forces which were outside the human psyche.

Mirror Worship in India

"Mirror worship"—what is it? A man looks into a mirror and sees his own image. He worships his own image thinking that he is the God. Indians believe that "God is in everybody or everybody is God". An individual who can see the God in himself can never become human rights unfriendly. For, a person who sees God in himself sees the same God in others. He recognizes equality among human beings. Study the developments just before Magna Carta, or during the French Revolution or during the American Revolution and connect them to the development of human rights consciousness in the west. Study the independence movements in India and see how non-violent were they? Indians fought against the British and got freedom. Indians achieved their freedom through non-violence and they could do so because they were guided by a philosophy which believed in human values and fundamental human rights. The mystic values were there to guide the people of India.

There is an allegation against some of the human rights activists in the west. For, they think that they alone are human rights friendly and all others are human rights unfriendly. They think so and say so because they are unable to understand the

Indian concepts on human rights. The right to divorce may be a human right for the westerners, but is a curse for Indians. Marriage is a sacrament for Indians and therefore, they find it difficult to accept/think of the rights on dissolution of marriage as human rights. I have seen some foreign human rights activists arguing for establishing human rights in the way they want them to be established. The attitude of "WE ARE O.K. and YOU ARE NOT O.K." is seen among some of the westerners. I used to tell them: "Look, the Universal Declaration of Human Rights came into existence in 1948. Now more than half a century has elapsed since the Universal Declaration has been passed. It is time now to see whether or not the articles contained in the Declaration need a revision. For, they were written by human beings, but the revealed truths were given by the Almighty. Revelations are superior to human intellect or intellectual abstractions. More may have to be added to the existing Universal Declaration and some may have to be deleted. There is no eternal sanctity for any man-made human rights laws, Conventions or Declarations passed by the United Nations. Laws are dynamic and are changing whereas the inspired truths of the seers and sages are eternal. They do not get changed. "Who am I? Who are others?"—These questions were asked by the *ṛsis* and mystics in India. They got revelation. The same questions were asked by many in all parts of the world—by Confucius and Lao Tze. The answers to the questions are seen in the sacred writings of Israel as also in the *Avesta*. The answers to the questions are given in the preaching of Tirthankara and Buddha. No doubt, the answers are found in the poetry of Homer and in the tragedies of Euripides and Sophocles. Plato and Aristotle gave answers to the questions. And all of them were talking about human rights and the necessity of respecting the human persons. Therefore, I used to tell the foreign human rights activists to go deep into the inspired truths of Indian mysticism and appreciate them. I used to tell them that they must study the world religions, revealed truths and great philosophies and they do not say anything more than what is seen in the teachings of great seers and mystics. All of them teach that every man is a microcosm—he has relationship with other human beings—and all human beings share a common destiny. The Indian mysticism spoke the same thing for many thousands of years and the human rights activists started telling loudly about man's worth and dignity recently, but with a pride—with a pride that the west is the birth place of human rights. They started to present, to some extent, their own partial and imperfect views on human rights as the complete or total of human rights. They failed to show respect to human rights in their wholeness as they existed in other parts of the world. The western human rights activist, in their one-sided concern to accept human rights purely from their subjective angle, seem to have forgotten that men and women always—everywhere in the world—move towards a truth which transcends them. This is seen in the west as well as in the east. But, they seem to ignore this truth and tend even to devalue it. The result has been that the people in the east started to look to the west to know more about human rights. Some people are found to distrust the truths revealed to them by the *ṛsis* and mystics.

I have listened to many lectures delivered by very learned scholars, judges, jurists and so on about human rights. And I find them speaking on human rights looking to the west—as if the concept of human rights is the contribution of the west to the world. I have seen in TV the heads of certain countries going to another country and preach about human rights. Miserably, they fail to take note of human rights violations taking place in their own countries. Terrorism, insurgency, State sponsored terrorism, atrocities committed on another countries' territory etc. are just forgotten by these human rights activists! Why? The reason is that they are ignorant about the inspired truths imparted by the God's seers and mystics. A change in man takes place only if there takes place a change in his soul and a change in one's soul occurs only if he is prepared to internalize the eternal truths about man, his dignity and worth. God's revelation is immersed in time and history and through this revelation, men and women are offered the ultimate truth about human rights. Any declaration or convention brought out by any organization cannot make people to become human rights friendly unless the people themselves are prepared to accept the truth in its wholeness. This wisdom of the mystical seers insists upon an open acceptance to the universality of the truth it bears. All human beings are equal in dignity and this truth has been told by the sages. Man is the only creature on earth who not only is capable of knowing this fact, but who knows he knows the truth. He should accept the truth and must practice it in life. In order to become human rights friendly, according to a free and rightly tuned will, he must set his foot upon the revelations of God and the revelations are seen in the mystics' writings. Revelations contain inspired truths and only true values can lead people to happiness.

I have little or very little information on eastern mysticisms and their contributions to the development of the concepts in human rights. At the same time, when one goes through the philosophies of the east, he may come across many thoughts having relationship with the modern concepts of human rights. On going through the philosophies of the east from the fourth millennium B.C. to the present day, one may see that the human mind is one and the same always at any time in human history. Human rights and human rights violations were there everywhere just as they are seen today. This is seen in Egypt, in Babylonia and Israel in the ancient past. Philosophy of Zoroaster speaks about it. Hinduism and Buddhism tell about it. The Chinese sages and Mohammed talk about it. What more do we require to subscribe to the view that human rights and human rights violations were seen from time antiquity.

> "Give bread to him who hath no field
> So shall thou gain a good name
> For the future for ever"

These lines are seen on the wall of the Theban tomb in Egypt (2000 B.C.?) and certainly it shows that the Egyptians believed in the right of man to live—and this is recognized as a human right today by the world community. Look into the Code of Hammurabi in Babylonia and there one finds rules and laws for asserting the rights of people against injustices done to them. In Israel, Moses gave ten commandments and they contained human rights. Zoroaster said: "About righteousness I consider my foremost distress; about righteousness my foremost endeavour; and for righteousness the tendency of my desire". Sages like Lao-Tze and Confucius taught the people a new way of life. Islam contains a number of principles in human rights. Hinduism and Buddhism are pregnant with human rights and their applications in daily life. The area—*i.e.*, mysticism and human rights—is worth researching. Philosophers of the west—say, Socrates, Plato, Aristotle, St. Augustine, Peter Abelard, St. Thomas Acquinas, Rane Descartes, Benedict Spinoza, Gottfried Leibniz, John Locke, George Berkeley, David Hume, Immanuel Kant, G.W. Hegel, Kirkegaard, Schopenhauer, Bergson, Dewey, Santayana and so on—have made their contributions to the development of human rights. Their contributions are not discussed here as they do not become the subject matter of this book. Nevertheless, one may emphatically say that the claims of certain people or countries to the fatherhood of human rights concepts are to be rejected. Human rights concepts have developed over a period of several thousands of years and the contributions of Indian sages and seers are really very great. But, the Indians do not get it. The reason is that Indians do not conduct any researches into this special area of human interest.

Conclusion

I have read a number of books—both Indian and foreign—on human rights. I have listened to a number of lectures on human rights, but I have never heard anyone talking on Indian mysticism and human rights. Therefore, I have sensed the need to connect Hindu mysticism and its relationship to human rights. The importance of the mystics' revelation in the development of human rights and its influence on the patterns of personal and social life and behaviour is there for all of us to see. In addition, the seers' vision exercises a powerful, though not always obvious, influence on human rights. For this reason, I have judged it appropriate and necessary to do some research on the subject and bring out a book emphasizing the value of inspired truths for understanding human rights as well as the false claims which some vested interests take to the fatherhood of human rights...They neglect or purposefully reject the truths of revelation in the development and propagation of human rights consciousness. I am profoundly convinced that Indian mysticism has decisively influenced the development of human rights consciousness. Nevertheless, I do not claim that my book is an exhaustive work in the area, yet my exercise is a powerful stimulus for many to pursue their search for a deeper understanding. A survey of the literature on human rights, especially in the west, shows that the writers did not have any insights into the *ṛsis*' contributions to the development of human rights. Some of them think that inspiration and revelation come in the domain of theology which, according to them, has nothing much to do with human rights. This indeed is an erroneous view for those who are not open to realities. Human dignity and the worth of human person—they form a part of theology. Human and humanizing meaning of human existence and God's design to have them in the human nature are seen in human development and its acceptance of human rights for all. Human rights and the police as they are seen in *Bharatiya* mysticism and U.N.'s Conventions must be appreciated from this perspective in mind—and with this perception in every sense.

Appendix

UNITED NATIONS' DOCUMENTS ON CRIME PREVENTION AND CRIMINAL JUSTICE

PART ONE

A. Standards of General Application

1. Declaration of the Fourth United Nations Congress on the Prevention of Crime and the Treatment of Offenders.
2. Report of the Sixth United Nations Congress on the Prevention of Crime and the Treatment of Offenders (General Assembly Resolution 35/171).
3. Adoption of the Milan Plan of Action.
4. Guiding Principles for Crime Prevention and Criminal Justice in the Context of Development and a New International Economic Order.
5. International Co-operation for Crime Prevention and Criminal Justice in the Context of Development (General Assembly Resolution 45/107).

B. International Co-operation

6. Prevention and control of organized crime.
7. Terrorist criminal activities.

8. Model Treaty on Extradition (General Assembly Resolution 45/116).
9. Model Treaty on Mutual Assistance in Criminal Matters (General Assembly Resolution 45/117).
10. Model Treaty on the Transfer of Proceedings in Criminal Matters (General Assembly Resolution 45/118).
11. Model Treaty for the prevention of crimes that infringe on the cultural heritage of peoples in the form of movable property.

C. Treatment of Offenders

12. World social situation [Economic and Social Council Resolution 663 (XXIV)].
13. Procedures for the effective implementation of the Standard Minimum Rules for the Treatment of Prisoners (Economic and Social Council Resolution 1984/47).
14. Model agreement on the Transfer of Foreign Prisoners and Recommendations on the treatment of foreign prisoners.
15. Basic Principles for the Treatment of Prisoners (General Assembly Resolution 45/111).
16. United Nations Standard Minimum Rules for Non-custodial Measures (The Tokyo Rules) (General Assembly Resolution 45/110).
17. Model Treaty on the Transfer of Supervision of Offenders Conditionally Sentenced or Conditionally Released (General Assembly Resolution 45/119).
18. Code of Conduct for Law Enforcement Officials (General Assembly Resolution 34/169).
19. Guidelines for the effective implementation of the Code of Conduct for Law Enforcement Officials (Economic and Social Council Resolution 1989/61).
20. Basic Principles on the Use of Force and Firearms by Law Enforcement Officials.
21. Basic Principles on the Independence of the Judiciary.

22. Procedures for the effective implementation of the Basic Principles on the Independence of the Judiciary (Economic and Social Council Resolution 1989/60).
23. Basic Principles on the Role of Lawyers.
24. Guidelines on the Role of Prosecutors.

D. Juvenile Justice

25. United Nations Standard Minimum Rules for the Administration of Juvenile Justice (The Beijing Rules) (General Assembly Resolution 40/33).
26. United Nations Standard Minimum Rules for the Administration of Juvenile Justice (The Beijing Rules) (Economic and Social Council Resolution 1989/66).
27. United Nations Guidelines for the Prevention of Juvenile Delinquency (The Riyadh Guidelines) (General Assembly Resolution 45/112).
28. United Nations Rules for the Protection of Juveniles Deprived of their Liberty (General Assembly Resolution 45/113).

E. Protection of Victims

29. Declaration of Basic Principles of Justice for Victims of Crimes and Abuse of Power (General Assembly Resolution 40/340).
30. Implementation of the Declaration of Basic Principles of Justice for Victims of Crime and Abuse of Power (Economic and Social Council Resolution 1989/57).
31. Victims of crime and abuse of power (Economic and Social Council Resolution 1990/22).
32. Protection of the human rights of victims of crime and abuse of power.

F. Capital Punishment

33. Capital punishment [General Assembly Resolution 2857 (XXVI)].

34. Safeguards guaranteeing protection of the rights of those facing the death penalty (Economic and Social Council Resolution 1984/50).
35. Implementation of the safeguards guaranteeing protection of the rights of those facing the death penalty (Economic and Social Council Resolution 1989/64).
36. Capital punishment (Economic and Social Council Resolution 1990/29).

G. Torture and Other Cruel, Inhuman or Degrading Treatment or Punishment; Extra-Legal Executions

37. Declaration on the Protection of All Persons from Being Subjected to Torture and Other Cruel, Inhuman or Degrading Treatment or Punishment.
38. Effective prevention and investigation of extra-legal, arbitrary and summary executions (Economic and Social Council Resolution 1989/65).

H. Convention for the Suppression of the Traffic in Persons and of the Exploitation of the Prostitution of others

39. Convention for the Suppression of the Traffic in Persons and of the Exploitation of the Prostitution of Others.

PART TWO

HUMAN RIGHTS

1. Universal Declaration of Human Rights.
2. International Covenant on Economic, Social and Cultural Rights.
3. International Covenant on Civil and Political Rights.
4. Optional Protocol to the International Covenant on Civil and Political Rights.
5. Second Optional Protocol to the International Covenant on Civil and Political Rights, aiming at the abolition of

the death penalty (General Assembly Resolution 44/128).

6. Convention against Torture and Other Cruel, Inhuman or Degrading Treatment or Punishment (General Assembly Resolution 39/46).
7. Principles of Medical Ethics relevant to the Role of Health Personnel, particularly Physicians, in the Protection of Prisoners and Detinues against Torture and Other Cruel, Inhuman or Degrading Treatment or Punishment.
8. Body of principles for the Protection of All Persons under any Form of Detention or Imprisonment (General Assembly Resolution 43/173).
9. Convention on the Rights of the Child (General Assembly Resolution 44/25).

Bibliography

Advaita Ashrama (Publisher), *A Bridge to Eternity,* Advaita Ashrama, Calcutta, 1986.

Basu, Durga Dass, *Human Rights in Constitutional Law,* Prentice Hall, New Delhi, 1994.

Burke, Marie Louise, *Swami Vivekananda in the West: New Discoveries,* Advaita Ashrama, Calcutta, 1983.

Carey, John, *International Protection of Human Rights,* Oceana Publications, Inc., New York, 1968.

Das, Kamleshwar, *Human Rights and the United Nations,* Ind. Yearbook of Intl. Affairs, 1956.

Donnelly, Jack, *International Human Rights,* Westview Press, London, 1993.

Date, V.H., *Upanisads Retold,* Allied Publishers Pvt. Ltd., Bombay, 1979.

Donnelly, Jack, *Concept of Human Rights,* Croomhelm, London, 1985.

Goel, Aruna, *Indian Philosophy: Nyaya-Vaisesika and Modern Science,* Sterling Publishers Pvt. Ltd., Delhi, 1984.

Hiriyenna, M., *Essentials of Indian Philosophy,* Blackie & Son Publishers Pvt. Ltd., Bombay, 1973.

Kalalah, A.B., *Human Rights in International Law,* ed. by. T.R. Subramanya, New Delhi, 1986.

Lauterpacht, H., *International Law and Human Rights,* Archon Books, 1968.

McDougal, M.S. and Geehard Bebb, Human Rights and United Nations, 58, *American Journal of International Law*, 1964.

Mathew, K.K., Human Rights: Basis and Limits, *Eastern Journal of International Law*, 1978.

Mookerjee, Nanda, *Sri Ramakrishna in the Eyes of Brahma and Christian Admirers,* Firma Klm Pvt. Ltd., Calcutta, 1976.

Nair, Balakrishnan, *Srimad Bhagavad Gita: Sivaravindam Maha Bhashyam,* (Mal. version), State Institute of Languages, Thiruvananthapuram, 1995.

Nair, P.S., *Sampoorna Ramayanam,* Vidyarambham Publishers, Allappuzha, 1996.

Namboothiripad, Narayanan, O.M.C., *Ṛg Veda,* (Mal. version) Vol. I, D.C. Books, Kottayam, 1995.

Namboothiripad, Narayanan, O.M.C., *Ṛg Veda* (Mal. Ver.), Vol. II, D.C. Books, Kottayam, 1995.

Namboothiripad, Narayanan, O.M.C., *Ṛg Veda* (Mal. Ver.), Vol. III, D.C. Books, Kottayam, 1995.

Namboothiripad, Narayanan, O.M.C., *Ṛg Veda* (Mal. Ver.), Vol. IV, D.C. Books, Kottayam, 1995.

Namboothiripad, Narayanan, O.M.C., *Ṛg Veda* (Mal. Ver.), Vol. V, D.C. Books, Kottayam, 1995.

Namboothiripad, Narayanan, O.M.C., *Ṛg Veda* (Mal. Ver.), Vol. VI, D.C. Books, Kottayam, 1995.

Namboothiripad, Narayanan, O.M.C., *Ṛg Veda* (Mal. Ver.), Vol. VII & VIII, D.C. Books, Kottayam, 1995.

Pandey, Rama, S., Development: Peace and Human Rights in South Asia, *Indian Journal of Social Work,* 54(4), Oct. 1993.

Paul, Sieghart, *International Law of Human Rights,* Mittal, New Delhi, 1990.

Prabhupada, A.C. Bhaktivedanta Swami, *Sri Isopanisad,* ISCON Press, Boston, 1969.

Radhakrishnan and J.H. Muirhead (eds.). *Contemporary Indian Philosophy,* George Allen & Unwin Ltd., New York, 1966.

Ramakrishna Math (Publisher), *The Bṛhadaranyaka Upanisad,* Sri Ramakrishna Math, Mylapore, 1968.

Sarma, Sankara, M., *Kalisantharanopanishad,* Kizhakedath Mana, Kalady, 1988.

Sreenivasan, Kasthuri, *Tirukkural,* Bharatiya Vidya Bhavan, Bombay, 1969.

Swami Chinmayananda, *Discourses on Kenopanishad,* Chinmaya Mission, Madras, 1961.

Swami, Mridananda (Commentary), *Mundakopanishad,* Sri

Ramakrishna Math, Trichur, 1993.

Swami, Mridananda (Commentary), *Kathopanishad,* Sri Ramakrishna Math, Trichur, 1993.

Swami, Mridananda (Commentary), *Svetasvataropanishad,* Sri Ramakrishna Math, Trichur, 1994.

Swami, Mridananda (Commentary), *Taittiriyopanishad,* Sri Ramakrishna Math, Trichur, 1994.

Swami, Mridananda (Commentary), *Kenopanishad,* Sri Ramakrishna Math, Trichur, 1995.

Swami, Mridananda (Commentary), Mundukyopanishad, Sri Ramakrishna Math, Trichur, 1995.

Swami Mumukshananda, *Selections from the Complete Works of Swami Vivekananda,* Advaita Ashrama, Calcutta, 1997.

Swami Nikhilananda, *The Upanishads: A New Translation* (Vol. I), Bonanza Books, New York, 1949.

Swami Ranganathananda, *A Pilgrim looks at the World* (Vol. II), Bharatiya Vidya Bhavan, Bombay, 1975.

Swami Ranganathananda, *The Message of the Upanishads,* Bharatiya Vidya Bhavan, Bombay, 1968.

Swami Saradananda, Sri Ramakrishna: *The Great Master,* Sri Ramakrishna Math, Mylapore, 1952.

Swami Sarvananda, *Mundakopanishad,* Sri Ramakrishna Math, Mylapore, 1974.

Swami Sarvananda, *Taittiriyopanishad,* Sri Ramakrishna Math, Mylapore, 1958.

Swami Tapasyananda, (Tr). *Srimad Bhagavata: The Holy Book of God,* Sri Ramakrishna Math, Madras, 1982.

Swami Tejasananda, *Swami Vivekananda and his Message* Ramakrishna Mission Saradapitha, Howrah, 1972.

Swami Vidyatmananda (ed.), *Atman Alone Abides,* Sri Ramakrishna Math, Madras, 1978.

Thamilmaran, V.T., *Human Rights in Third World Perspective,* Haranad Publishing House, Delhi, 1992.

Thampuran, Kodungalloor Kunjukuttan, *Srimahabharatam,* Vols. I, II, III, IV, V, VI, VII (Mal. Ver.), Sahithya Pravarthaka Cooperative Society Ltd., Kottayam, 1981.

Vadackumchery, James, (ed.), *Police and Human Rights,* Kerala

Police Officers' Association, Thiruvananthapuram, 1994.

Vadackumchery, James, *Human Rights and The Police in India,* A.P.H. Publishing Corporation, Delhi, 1996.

Vadackumchery, James, *Human Rights Friendly Police: A Myth or Reality?* A.P.H. Publishing Corporation, Delhi, 2000.

Will, Gordon L., The Evolution of the European Convention of Human Rights, 57, *American Journal of International Law,* 1963.

Yale, John, *What Religion is in the Words of Swami Vivekananda,* Phoenix House Ltd., London, 1962.

Yati, Nitya Chaitanya, *The Bṛhadaranyaka Upanishad,* (Mal. Ver.). D.C. Books, Kottayam, 1996.

INDEX